So you really want t

History

Britain 1750–c.1900

Answer Book

Bob Pace M.A.

Series Editor: Niall Murphy M.A. (Cantab)

GALORE PARK

www.galorepark.co.uk

Published by Galore Park Publishing Ltd
19/21 Sayers Lane, Tenterden, Kent TN30 6BW
www.galorepark.co.uk

Typography by Typetechnique, London W1
Printed by Charlesworth Press, Wakefield

ISBN: 978 1 905735 57 0

First published 2012

Details of other Galore Park publications are available at www.galorepark.co.uk

ISEB Revision Guides, publications and examination papers may also be obtained from Galore Park.

Contents

Introduction

The suggested answers in this book are designed to be informative rather than prescriptive and should be used as a guide on what to look for in and how to assess an answer. The accompanying marks for the essay questions reflect the ISEB Common Entrance mark scheme.

The appendix at the back contains a copy of the ISEB Commom Entrance mark scheme.

Chapter 1 The Seven Years' War

Exercise 1.1

Fighting between the French and British American colonies often occurred because of wars breaking out in **Europe**. *But in 1754 it was the actions of a young colonial officer named* **George Washington** *that started a war. The French had built Fort* **Duquesne** *and this was seen as a threat by the British. A force under the command of General* **Braddock** *was sent to take it. Just 6 miles from the fort they were* **ambushed** *by a small force of* **French** *and* **Native Americans**. *The British were defeated because the attackers* **hid** *in the trees and tall grass while the British troops stood in* **dense ranks**. *What was left of the British force was led in retreat by* **Washington**.   (10 marks)

Exercise 1.2

The paragraph should include a clear introduction, argument and conclusion. The better answers will not simply list the main long and short-term factors but will also show how these factors link or connect to each other. The most effective paragraphs will also point out the most important reason for the British defeat and create an argument to support this. The paragraph should cover the following points:

- *There are a number of reasons for the defeat of General Braddock's army at the Battle of Monongahela River.*

- *Probably the most important reason was poor British leadership.*

- *General Braddock attempted to fight the campaign as he would in Europe. His army was ill prepared to fight in an ambush.*

- *During the actual battle Braddock tried to stop his men from taking to the trees to fight the French and Native Americans, instead insisting on shoulder-to-shoulder firing that left the British easy targets for their enemies. Because of this a smaller force of French and Native Americans defeated Braddock's army and forced it to retreat.*

- *In conclusion Braddock's poor leadership lead to the conditions that brought a British defeat at the Battle of Monongahela River.*   (10 marks)

Exercise 1.3

Good answers for this exercise should clearly identify each person and his role in the Seven Years' War.

George Washington: *A young Virginian militia officer, Washington unintentionally started the war with his attack upon the French and his defeat at Fort Necessity. He played a key role in saving what was left of Braddock's army after its defeat at the Battle of Monongahela River.*

(3 marks)

General Braddock: *Braddock was a British commander sent to lead a force to take the French Fort Duquesne. He was brave but unfamiliar with frontier/wilderness fighting and led his army into an ambush at the Battle of Monongahela where he was killed and his army defeated.*

(3 marks)

William Pitt the Elder: *Pitt was a British politician and brilliant speaker who used his position of Secretary of State to create a winning war strategy for the Seven Years' War. He helped Prussia to fight in Europe while using the British Navy and Army to focus on defeating France in the colonies.*

(3 marks)

Marquis de Montcalm: *A French commander in America, Montcalm proved a dangerous opponent for the British. He had a number of successes, such as taking Fort William Henry and defeating the British at Ticonderoga, but was defeated and killed outside Quebec at the Battle of the Plains of Abraham.*

(3 marks)

General James Wolfe: *Wolfe was one of the younger commanders Pitt the Elder used to win the war in America. He was given command of the British forces attacking Quebec. His success at the Battle of the Plains of Abraham led to the fall of Quebec but he lost his life during the battle.*

(3 marks)

Total for exercise: 15 marks

Exercise 1.4

The description of the campaign for Quebec in 1759 should cover the following points:

- *Quebec was the capital of French Canada.*
- *Quebec was difficult to reach and attack because it was built on cliffs, bounded by rivers and well defended.*
- *The British force sailed up the St Lawrence River and seized the high ground across the river from the city.*
- *The commander of the fleet, Admiral Saunders, sailed past Quebec's warships to operate south of the city.*
- *Wolfe's attack at Montmorency Falls failed, with the loss of 480 men.*
- *Under siege, the French troops in Quebec ran short of supplies. Montcalm planned to hold out until winter when the river would freeze and the British fleet would be forced to leave.*

- *Wolfe kept the French guessing by moving his troops up and down the river. He also kept his plans to land and climb the cliff at Anse au Foulon from his own men until the last moment.*

- *At the Battle of the Plains of Abraham, the British soldiers had an advantage over the French and their native allies on open ground. Attacks on the British flanks were driven back by British light infantry. Montcalm's troops were defeated and Montcalm killed; Wolfe also lost his life in the battle.*

- *Quebec surrendered on 18th September. When Montreal also fell, French Canada was no more.* (20 marks)

Exercise 1.5

1. *Wolfe was wounded by 'three balls through his body'.* (2 marks)

2. *The writer says that Wolfe was a hero ('a sacrifice to the glory of your country') and will be remembered for his qualities and his actions ('your virtues and your exploits').* (3 marks)

3. *Source C represents the death of Wolfe as a sad but glorious moment. This clearly agrees with A ('brave General Wolfe') and with B ('you have fallen a sacrifice ... to your country').* (7 marks)

4. A good answer will look at all the sources and refer to both their content and provenance. It should cover the following points:

   - *All of these sources have their use for a historian.*

   - *Source A, a contemporary newspaper report from the British colonies, shows how the American colonists of the time saw Wolfe's death as heroic, although it may not be very accurate.*

   - *Source B is another contemporary view of Wolfe's death and even though it is made up it shows how many people in Britain saw Wolfe as a great hero.*

   - *Source C, being a painting, is inevitably influenced by the feelings of the artist and whoever ordered it but it is regarded as fairly accurate and again shows the popular belief that Wolfe was a great hero.*

     (8 marks)

Total for exercise: 20 marks

Exercise 1.6

Key factors for the success of this essay are how well it has been organised and how successful the pupil has been in analysing and showing judgement. Simply listing factors will show little judgement; organising them into categories such as long and short-term clearly shows more. Crucial to successful writing here is an attempt by the pupil to show how the various consequences link or connect to each other. This can be most clearly done by developing an argument about the most important or far-reaching consequence or consequences.

Short-term consequences of the Seven Years' War for Britain and its Empire:

- *These seemed to be largely good.*
- *France had been truly defeated and stripped of its possessions in America.*
- *This ended the threat of French attack on the English American colonies and presented them with the chance to develop to the benefit of the Empire.*
- *Britain's navy now controlled the seas.*

Long-term consequences:

- *The Seven Years' War led to a number of troubles for Britain.*
- *The great debt caused by the war brought conflict in the American colonies.*
- *Much of Europe now feared the great power of Britain.*
- *Both of these factors were a great threat to Britain in the 1770s, when the American War of Independence broke out.*
- *This could be argued as the more important consequence of the British victory in the Seven Years' War.* (10 marks)

Chapter 2 The American Rebellion and world war

Exercise 2.1

The Proclamation of 1763: *This was an attempt to prevent the spread of the American colonies westwards and established rules for relations with the Native American tribes. That and its protection of Catholicism in Canada made it highly unpopular with the colonists and impossible to enforce.* (3 marks)

The Stamp Tax: *In order to raise money to pay Britain's debt from the Seven Years' War, legal documents, newspapers, playing cards and dice had to carry a stamp that had been bought from the British government. Groups of colonists objected to the tax, declaring that only representatives of the people had the right to impose taxes, and boycotted British goods.* (3 marks)

Sons of Liberty: *Active in the late 1760s and into the 1770s, the Sons of Liberty were formed in Boston, Massachusetts, in response to the Stamp Act. They saw themselves as 'patriots' who were not above using violence to achieve their ends, for example, using intimidation to prevent people from selling the stamps.* (3 marks)

The Townshend Duties: *Passed in 1767, the Townsend Duties were a set of taxes on goods such as paint, paper, glass and tea, intended to gather money from the colonies and also to show that Britain was in control. In response, the colonials boycotted British goods and there was violence against customs officials.*

Samuel Adams: *Adams was a former tax collector who, as leader of the Sons of Liberty, urged the Massachusetts Assembly to declare the Townshend Duties illegal. This declaration led to friction between soldiers and some citizens of Boston, and to a propaganda war between the Patriots, who backed Adams, and the Loyalists, who supported the government.* (3 marks)

The Boston Massacre: *In early March 1770, as a result of tensions over the Townshend Duties, a group of local men and boys taunted the British soldiers on sentry duty. A shot was fired and the soldiers fired into the crowd, hitting 11 men and killing five. Adams and the Patriots branded this 'the Boston Massacre' and used it to whip up anti-British feelings, although the solders involved were found not guilty of murder.* (3 marks)

The Boston Tea Party: *In 1773, the Tea Act was passed. The Patriots resented this tax and on 16th December 1773 decided to take direct action. Disguised as Native Americans, they destroyed and threw overboard the cargo of three tea ships waiting to be unloaded in Boston.*

The British Parliament was outraged; the dispute was no longer about tea, but about the right to rule the colonies. (3 marks)

The Coercive Acts: Following the Boston Tea Party and other actions by the American Patriots, the British Parliament passed a set of acts designed to bring the colonials to heel. The port of Boston was to be closed, a military governor named General Gage was to take over and the authority of the colonial assembly would be reduced. In response, Adams and other Patriots summoned the colonies to send delegates to a first meeting of a Continental Congress. (3 marks)

Total for exercise: 21 marks

Exercise 2.2

(a) The answer should make good use of the available information and present a clear viewpoint, either in support of the Patriots or defending the position of the British Crown. For the less able, a framework could be established to enable a full piece of writing. Depending on the event chosen, articles should cover the following points:

The Boston Massacre

- *Taxes passed by the British government to pay their debts from the Seven Years' War led to tensions between the British and the American colonials, who believed that only the local colonial assemblies had the right to impose taxes on the colonies.*

- *In 1767 the British government passed the Townshend Duties, to raise money and tighten up Britain's control over the colonies. American Patriots responded by boycotting British goods and declaring the Duties illegal.*

- *Several regiments of British troops were sent to Boston to impose the Duties and friction developed between the soldiers and some citizens of Boston.*

- *On an evening in March 1770, a group of local men and boys began to taunt the British soldiers on sentry duty outside the Customs House in Boston.*

- *A shot was fired, possibly by a member of the crowd, possibly by a soldier.*

- *The soldiers, thinking they were under attack, fired into the crowd, hitting 11 men and killing three; two more later died of their wounds.*

- *The Patriots branded this 'the Boston Massacre' and accused the British of deliberately murdering colonials, using it to whip up anti-British feeling. The soldiers involved were tried and found not guilty.* (15 marks) or:

The Boston Tea Party

- *Although the Townshend Duties were repealed, a tax on tea was retained to maintain the British government's right to impose taxes on the American colonies. The government decided to sell millions of tons of East India tea to the colonies at knock-down prices, in order to boost the funds of the East India Company and to raise money through import tax.*

- *The Patriots resented the imposition of taxes from London and the Tea Act of 1773 sparked a major confrontation. The Patriots demanded 'no taxation without representation' and on 16th December 1773 decided to take direct action.*

- *Wearing blankets to disguise themselves as Native Americans, about 200 Patriots boarded three tea ships waiting to unload in Boston harbour, and destroyed and threw overboard their cargo.*

- *In response, the British government passed a set of acts, called 'the Coercive Acts' by the Patriots, designed to strengthen Britain's rule in the colonies and reduce the influence of the colonials.*

- *This led Samuel Adams and other Patriots to form the Continental Congress, a meeting of delegates from many of the colonies.* (15 marks)

(b) The cartoon should demonstrate an understanding of the viewpoint of either the Patriots or the British Parliament. (15 marks)

Total for exercise: 30 marks

Exercise 2.3

Fighting at Lexington and Concord	April 1775
Battle of Bunker Hill	June 1775
American attack on Canada fails	May 1776
The Declaration of Independence	July 1776
Americans driven out of New York	August 1776
Washington attacks Trenton and Princeton	December 1776
Battles at Saratoga	September–October 1777
British success in the southern colonies	1778–1780
Cornwallis fails to crush General Greene	March 1781
British surrender at Yorktown	October 1781 (10 marks)

Exercise 2.4

General Thomas Gage: *Gage was the military governor of Massachusetts. In 1775 he led British attacks on Lexington and Concord, seizing American supplies but ultimately finding himself and his army trapped by the rebel militia.* (3 marks)

General William Howe: *Howe sent a large British force to the Battle of Bunker Hill, securing British control of the Charlestown peninsula. In July 1776 he attacked New York, driving out Washington and winning several battles. In 1777 he seized Philadelphia, but failed to destroy Washington's army. Howe resigned following the surrender of Burgoyne.* (3 marks)

General John Burgoyne: *Burgoyne played a key role in the Saratoga campaign of 1777. He planned to march south from Quebec and cut off the New England colonies from the rest of the 13 colonies. His forces captured Ticonderoga, Hubbarbton and Fort Edward, but ran into difficulties at Bemis Heights when they were attacked by American riflemen; they drove off the attack but were later driven back and surrendered on 17th October.* (3 marks)

George Washington: *Washington was commander of the Continental Army forces surrounding Boston. His successes at Trenton and Princeton in 1776 raised the morale of his army and, despite being defeated by Howe in several battles, in 1781 his men and the French force under General Rochambeau forced the British to surrender at Yorktown. Although not a particularly good battlefield commander, Washington's political skills kept many colonies firmly opposed to British rule.* (3 marks)

General Lord Cornwallis: *The commander of the main British force in the south, Cornwallis tried to crush the rebellion in the southern colonies while the largest part of the British army in America guarded New York. At first the campaigns in the south went well for Britain, but when his supplies ran low and his soldiers fell ill, and under threat from General Greene's American forces, Cornwallis decided to march north. He established a base at Chesapeake Bay but, following the Battle of the Capes, his army were trapped in Yorktown and surrendered on 19th October 1781.* (3 marks)

General Benedict Arnold: *Arnold played a key role in the battles at Saratoga, persuading General Gates to unleash riflemen on Burgoyne's troops at Freeman's Farm, and driving back the British and German forces at the Battle of Bemis Heights. However, unhappy with what he felt was a lack of recognition of his achievements and abilities, he changed sides and was treated as a traitor by the colonials.* (3 marks)

Lord Germain: *A member of Lord North's government, Germain was in charge of the war's strategy. He approved Bugoyne's plan to attack from Canada but his orders that General Howe should march up the Hudson River valley from New York to support Burgoyne reached Howe late and were ignored.*

General Horatio Gates: *Gates was the victorious American army commander at Saratoga but was defeated by the British during their initially successful campaign in the southern colonies.* (3 marks)

Total for exercise: 21 marks

Exercise 2.5

1. *The figures in the foreground are not in uniform; it is known from other accounts that the militia suffered causalities and the British did not.* (2 marks)

2. *According to Source B, the commanding British officer first aggressively 'accosted' the militia, ordering them to 'disperse' and saying 'damn you'. The British troops then shot at the militia, the officers firing first ('one or two officers discharged their pistols') and then the soldiers ('the firing of 4 or 5 of the soldiers, and then there seemed to be a general discharge').* (3 marks)

3. A Level Two answer will connect B to one of the other sources; a Level Three answer will consider all three sources, concluding that Sources A and B generally do not agree about the role of the British troops. (7 marks)

4. A good answer will look at all the sources and refer to both their content and provenance. It should cover the following points:

   - *The picture was painted in 1883 and so is not contemporary, and probably reflects the feelings of the artist and whoever commissioned the picture. It may not be an accurate depiction of events.*

   - *Source A, a contemporary newspaper report, could be considered propaganda as it was printed in a Massachusetts newspaper. It therefore shows the American Patriots' view of events, but is not necessarily very accurate.*

   - *Source B is another contemporary view, written by a British commander in Boston. Some of the details are probably accurate, but is most useful in understanding the official British view of the events, rather than the events themselves.* (8 marks)

Total for exercise: 20 marks

Exercise 2.6

(a) The description of the Saratoga campaign should give a brief narrative of the reasons for the campaign, followed by a clear account of the events leading the surrender of Burgoyne's forces. A Level Three answer will be written with accuracy and an understanding of how certain decisions and events led to the eventual result. It should cover the following points:

- *Burgoyne planned to cut off the New England colonies from the rest of the 13 colonies, aided by General Howe. However, the order to Howe instructing him to support Burgoyne was sent too late.*

- *Burgoyne's forces captured Ticonderoga, Hubbardton and then Fort Edward.*

- *Burgoyne decided to launch a three-pronged attack on the American entrenchment at Bemis Heights. The densely forested terrain made it difficult for the three columns to co-operate, but was perfect for American riflemen, who attacked the British at Freeman's Farm. Burgoyne's men were under serious threat but managed to drive off the attack with support from General Riedesel's troops.*

- *After the battle, Burgoyne decided to entrench, but his supply route to Quebec had been cut and he grew short of supplies.*

- *On 7th October, Burgoyne sent a force to harvest wheat from nearby farms, but they were driven back by colonial troops under Arnold. The colonial attack was halted when Arnold was wounded in the leg, but on 17th October Burgoyne's army surrendered.* (20 marks)

(b) The explanation of the consequences of the Saratoga campaign for the British needs to display analytical skills and show judgement. This can be done by either breaking down the consequences into short and long-term and/or by arguing that one consequence, such as the entry of the French into the war, was the most important or decisive. The consequences identified could include the following:

Short-term consequences:

- *Burgoyne's defeat left General Howe in control of only Philadelphia, New York and part of Rhode Island; Howe resigned soon afterwards.*

- *A new strategy was needed; the new commander of British forces in America, General Clinton, decided on a campaign in the southern colonies.*

- *France had been quietly supplying the colonials with funds and equipment but the victory at Saratoga encouraged France to join the war against Britain openly, soon to be followed by Spain and the Netherlands.*

Long-term consequences:

- *Unfortunately, Loyalists were not as numerous in the south as the British hoped and, despite initial successes, ultimately the campaign in the southern colonies failed.*

- *The flow of French aid, and the eventual arrival of French troops and ships, kept the Patriot cause alive during the following years.*

- *The involvement of other European countries caused the war to expand, turning a colonial rebellion in America into an assault upon British holdings across the globe.*

(10 marks)

Chapter 3 The French Revolution and the Napoleonic Wars

Exercise 3.1

1. A good answer will pick out several points such as the eating of bodies, the hanging bodies, sitting on bodies, etc. (3 marks)

2. A good answer will refer to the crown treasures shown in the cartoon and the clear depictions of beheading shown by drawings. (3 marks)

3. A good answer will note the extreme exaggerations shown, including the pun on Sans Culottes, the cannibalism, etc. (5 marks)

4. A number of examples can be drawn upon; reasons such as the lack of food for the French in comparison with the British should be given. (5 marks)

5. *Such cartoons were printed and distributed throughout Britain as propaganda, with the aim of encouraging fear and/or mockery of the French, in order to prevent revolution in Britain.* (4 marks)

Total for exercise: 20 marks

Exercise 3.2

In the year **1789** revolution broke out in France. This happened because France was **bankrupt**. Leading the rebellion at first were the **middle class**. Many Britons thought France was going to become a **constitutional monarchy** like Britain. Some also believed this new age would bring **revolution** for Britain. But men like **Edmund Burke** feared that the French Revolution was leading to **political chaos**. When France declared **war** against Great Britain the Prime Minister, **William Pitt the Younger**, tried to stamp out radical ideas. (10 marks)

Exercise 3.3

Louis XVI: *King Louis XVI was absolute monarch of France when the French Revolution broke out in 1789. His government was bankrupt and he failed to deal with the problems of France. He was executed in 1793.* (3 marks)

Edmund Burke: *Burke was a Whig MP who feared the French Revolution and wrote a book, Reflections on the French Revolution, warning that it would end as a dictatorship.*

William Pitt the Younger: *Pitt was Prime Minister at the time of the French Revolution. To prevent revolution in Britain, his government encouraged and supported the Loyalists and took strong measures against reformers. The right of* habeas corpus *was suspended, meetings were banned unless permitted by local magistrates, the definition of treason was expanded and trade unions were made illegal. Pitt also encouraged other countries to join the war against France, offering British weapons and money.* (3 marks)

Habeas corpus: Habeas corpus *is the right to be charged and put on trial. During the wars against revolutionary France this right was suspended, meaning that people could be held indefinitely.* (3 marks)

Total for exercise: 12 marks

Exercise 3.4

Ships of the line	were the largest battleships in the navy.
According to Samuel Leech	a ship was made up of human machinery run by her captain.
The mess was	a group of sailors who ate together.
Bread was replaced by	ship's biscuit, often full of weevils.
Grog was	a mixture of rum and water.
While some sailors volunteered	many were impressed.
The cat o' nine tails	was used in flogging.
When at sea the crew	was usually divided into two watches.
Only the more senior officers	had any chance of privacy on board ship.
It is not true that	women did not sail on Royal Navy ships.

(10 marks)

Exercise 3.5

1. *Jeanette could not bear to be parted from her husband ('she was married, and quit her husband could not endure the thought').* (2 marks)

2. *Jeanette was lucky to survive because the ship was on fire ('the* Achille *which was burnt and blew up') and when she managed to swim to spar one of the French sailors forced her away ('bit and kicked her till she was obliged to quit') and had to swim to another.* (3 marks)

3. *All three sources show or describe Jeanette being rescued by boat from the water, but while Sources A and B refer to her nakedness when brought on board, C shows her clothed. The picture does not make it clear which ship's boat picked her up or where she was taken.* (7 marks)

4. A good answer will look at all the sources and refer to both their content and provenance. It should cover the following points:

    - *Source A is written by an eyewitness on board ship, but a common sailor.*

    - *Source B is an eyewitness account from an officer and is more based on fact than rumour.*

    - *Source C is possibly contemporary but is based on the story rather than on eyewitness accounts; it helps us understand how the public might have learned about the incident but does not really tell us what actually happened.* (8 marks)

    Total for exercise: 20 marks

Exercise 3.6

This narrative essay should show a sound grasp of the events of Nelson's life and also point out his strengths and weaknesses. A good answer will comment on what was his greatest strength and/or weakness, and also his greatest success. It should cover the following points:

- *The son of a clergyman, Horatio Nelson went to sea aged 12.*

- *He sustained various wounds during his career, including the loss of sight in one eye in Corsica in 1794, and the loss of his right arm in Tenerife in 1797.*

- *While in Naples, he met Emma Hamilton, who became his mistress until his death in 1805 and gave him one daughter.*

- *In the Battle of St Vincent in 1797, Nelson led his men to board and take two Spanish warships. He was hailed a British hero for his personal bravery and was soon promoted to Rear Admiral. During the battle, under Admiral Jervis, Nelson experienced a more disordered battle than the straight-line formation that was usually favoured, a tactic he was to remember.*

- *In 1798 Nelson attacked Napoleon's French fleet in the Mediterranean, destroying 11 of its 13 ships.*

- *In April 1801, Nelson attacked the Danish fleet in the Baltic, as part of a campaign to break up a new alliance between Russia, Sweden, Norway, Prussia and Denmark in support of France. He ignored an order to discontinue the attack from his more cautious commander, Admiral Parker, and the Danish fleet surrendered.*

- In 1805 Nelson was given the task of stopping the French-Spanish fleet from reaching the English Channel, but French Admiral Villeneuve evaded Nelson and anchored at Cadiz. Nelson sailed to Cadiz and on 21st October he defeated the French in the Battle of Trafalgar. His strategy was risky but he led by example. During the battle, Nelson was hit by a musket ball and died not long afterwards.

- Nelson's strengths included the loyalty he inspired in his men, his ability to think quickly and operate independently, his confidence in the superiority of his ships and crews, and his willingness to share his plans with his captains and trust them to react appropriately during battle (a quality known as 'the Nelson touch').

- Nelson was not always popular with his superiors, although he made sure they were well informed of his achievements and worked hard to gain favour with those in positions of power.

(20 marks)

Exercise 3.7

'Sepoy general': The term 'sepoy general' was used of Sir Arthur Wellesley, who served in India between 1796 and 1805, proving himself an excellent administrator and winning several battles. He was given the rank of Major-General and made a Knight of the Bath, but many British sneered at his successes.

(3 marks)

Continental System: The Continental System was Napoleon's attempt to bankrupt Britain by cutting off its trade with Europe. When Portugal refused to comply with the ban in 1807, a French army marched in and occupied the country; France similarly took over Spain in 1808, leading to the Peninsula War.

(3 marks)

Battle of Vimeiro: Sir Arthur Wellesley led an army to Portugal and on 21st August 1808 defeated the French at the Battle of Vimeiro. However, Sir Hew Dalrymple, who was commander of the expedition as a whole, then arrived and agreed a generous armistice with the defeated French general Junot; Dalrymple and Wellesley were summoned to Britain to face a court of inquiry.

(3 marks)

Torres Vedras: The Lines of Torres Vedras were impregnable fortifications in Portugal. In 1810 the Portuguese and British, under Wellesley, retreated behind the lines, taking with them all the civilians and food stocks of western Portugal, causing many of the French invasion forces to starve to death, before the rest retreated.

(3 marks)

Battle of Vitoria: In June 1813, Wellesley's army defeated the Spanish occupying forces at the Battle of Vitoria, clearing Spain of the enemy. Wellesley was rewarded with the rank of Field-Marshal.

(3 marks)

Congress of Vienna: *Following Napoleon's fall from power, the leaders of Europe called the Congress of Vienna, where they attempted to establish a new European order. Wellesley, now the Duke of Wellington, was one of the delegates.* (3 marks)

Total for exercise: **18 marks**

Exercise 3.8

The description of the battle should display a firm grasp of the chronology of the event. A good answer will show how the various factors and events were linked and identify, with supporting arguments, the key moments; the essay should end with a clear summary. Depending on the battle chosen, it should cover the following points:

Battle of Trafalgar

- *On 15th September 1805, Nelson sailed from Portsmouth for Cadiz, where French Admiral Villeneuve's fleet was awaiting orders from Napoleon.*

- *On 19th October, Villeneuve headed for the English Channel. The patrolling British frigates signalled to the waiting British fleet that the enemy had come out.*

- *The main British warships off Cape Trafalgar sighted the Franco-Spanish fleet at dawn on 21st October.*

- *Two columns of British ships, led by Nelson and Admiral Collingwood, sailed towards the enemy, intending to break their line. They came within firing range six hours after sighting the fleet.*

- *HMS Royal Sovereign, Collingwood's flagship, was the first to be fired on. For ten minutes she was unable to fire back, but succeeded in penetrating the enemy line and firing on the Spanish Santa Ana.*

- *At 12.45pm, Nelson's Victory passed between the French Bucentaure and the Redoubtable. She collided with the Redoubtable, and was fired on by the Neptune.*

- *The rest of the British columns joined the battles, while the front of the Franco-Spanish fleet continued on its way, only turning to join the battle when it was too late.*

- *The men on the Victory found themselves under musket fire from the Redoubtable, while the Victory's cannon smashed the Redoubtable's lower decks. At 1.15pm, Nelson was hit by a musket ball.*

- *By 2.15pm, something like 14 or 15 Franco-Spanish ships had surrendered. Nelson died not long after hearing the news.*

- *The battle petered out slowly as the British fleet and its 21 captured enemy ships sailed away.* (20 marks)

or:

Battle of Waterloo

- *Following the Battle of Quatre-Bras on 16th June, Wellington positioned his Anglo-Dutch army on a ridge at Mont-St. Jean, just south of the village of Waterloo, blocking the road to Brussels. Napoleon settled the majority of his army just to the south.*

- *On the morning of 18th June, Wellington's 68,000 men and 150 cannon were lined along the Mont-St. Jean ridge for nearly 2½ miles, with some of the best in three farms forward of the ridge: Hougoumont to the west, La Haye Sainte in the centre and Papelotte to the east.*

- *The French force numbered 72,000 men and 250 cannon. Napoleon decided to wait until about midday to begin the battle, to allow the ground to dry out from the previous night's rain.*

- *Napoleon's men prepared for an attack on the left centre of Wellington's line, intending to force him to retreat to the west, away from the Prussian reinforcements coming from the east.*

- *To distract Wellington, Napoleon first ordered an attack on Hougoumont on Wellington's right. This tactic later sucked in French reserves that should have been used elsewhere.*

- *At 1pm, the French cannon in the centre of the line opened fire. Soon afterwards, columns of French infantry advanced under Anglo-Dutch cannon fire. One Dutch brigade was pushed back, but the hole was blocked by British infantry. The French also attacked La Haye Sainte.*

- *At 2pm, British heavy cavalry charged and threw back the French infantry, although they suffered heavy casualties under a French cavalry counter-charge.*

- *At 4pm, mistaking Wellington's reorganisation of his troops for a retreat, French Marshal Ney began a series of cavalry assaults on the centre of the Anglo-Dutch line. Squares of infantry fought back, supported by artillery and light cavalry.*

- *By 6pm, the French had nearly broken Wellington's line. By now, the Prussians were attacking Napoleon's right flank. Without additional infantry support, the French cavalry attack failed. However, the French succeeded in taking La Haye Sainte.*

- *At 7pm, Napoleon unleashed his best men, the Imperial Guard units, on the Anglo-Dutch centre. Three columns advanced, under Allied cannon fire. When they reached the ridge, British fire-power at point-blank range forced them to retreat.*

- *Wellington ordered his men to advance and Napoleon's army fled the field of battle.*

(20 marks)

Exercise 3.9

The analysis of why the British won at Trafalgar or Waterloo, or of what was the important consequence of either of these victories, should include a discussion of the main causes or results. A good answer will either categorise them as short and long-term or will argue for one of them as the key factor. Look for an introduction that clearly states the pupil's argument; full and cogent conclusion is also needed. Depending on the essay chosen, it should cover the following points:

Britain's victory at Trafalgar

- *Nelson's bold tactic of using two columns of ships to break through the enemy's line, despite the fact that the leading British ships would be under enemy fire for some time before they could bring their own broadsides to bear on the enemy, split the Franco-Spanish fleet; British ships outnumbered portions of the enemy fleet and the leading Franco-Spanish ships did not turn to join the battle until it was too late.*

- *The French and Spanish gunners did not have enough training or experience to fire very effectively or rapidly; the rough seas made it more difficult to fire cannon accurately.*

Britain's victory at Waterloo

- *Napoleon's attack on Hougoumont got out of hand, sucking in French reserves that should have been used elsewhere.*

- *French Marshall Ney mistook Wellington's reinforcement of his troops for retreat. Instead of harrying a retreating foe, he found instead well-formed squares of the British infantry, supported by artillery and light cavalry.*

- *With Prussian reinforcements attacking his right flank, Napoleon did not send reinforcements to help Ney.*

- *Napoleon's Imperial Guard were forced back when Wellington's men fired on them at point-blank range.*

Consequences of the victory at Trafalgar

- *The Battle of Trafalgar prevented Napoleon from gaining control of the English Channel and invading Britain.*

- *The British Navy dominated the seas for more than a century.*

- *However, Pitt's plans to fight the French had failed to defeat Napoleon, and Nelson's death was a major blow.*

Consequences of the victory at Waterloo

- *Napoleon escaped from exile in Elba in 1815 and reclaimed power in France. The Allied leaders in Vienna declared war and Napoleon decided to try to defeat them one by one, beginning with the Prussian and Anglo-Dutch forces in Belgium.*

- *Napoleon could not survive the damage to his prestige caused by his defeat at Waterloo. He surrendered to the British on 15th July and was exiled to St Helena Island in the South Atlantic, where he died six years later.* (10 marks)

Chapter 4 Dissent and calls for political reform, 1815–1848

Exercise 4.1

Many working class people supported the calls for reform by the **radicals**. Times were hard at the end of the **Napoleonic** Wars because soldiers and sailors returned home to find there were no **jobs**. The price of bread was high because of an import tax put on foreign corn, the result of the **Corn Laws** of 1815.

Protests took a number of forms. The **Luddites/handloom workers** smashed mechanical looms that threatened their jobs. Great protest meetings were held about Parliament. One went terribly wrong in 1819 when **cavalry** charged the crowd. This event was quickly called the **Peterloo** massacre by the **radical** press. The government reacted by passing the **Six Acts**. In 1820 their fears seemed to come true with the discovery of the **Cato Street Conspiracy**. (10 marks)

Exercise 4.2

Thomas Paine: *A journalist and radical thinker, Paine called for greater representation for ordinary people.*

The Corn Laws of 1815: *Following the end of the Napoleonic Wars, British landowners were concerned that their profits would decrease now that cheap corn could be imported from abroad. The Corn Laws put an import tax on foreign corn, in order to protect the price of British corn. The tax on corn and other goods, needed to pay Britain's war debts, hit the poor hard.* (3 marks)

Luddites: *The term 'Luddites' was used to describe the handloom workers in the Midlands and north of England, who smashed up the new mechanical looms because they threatened their livelihoods.* (3 marks)

Peterloo: *On 16th August 1819, a large protest meeting was held in St Peter's Fields in Manchester, with the speaker Henry Hunt demanding changes in the way Parliament was elected and run. The local authorities panicked at the numbers and ordered a yeomen cavalry to break up the meeting; they charged with drawn swords, killing about a dozen and injuring hundreds of others. The event was dubbed 'Peterloo' by the radical press.* (3 marks)

The Six Acts: *The Six Acts of 1819 were passed by Lord Liverpool's Tory government in reaction to the radical calls for change. Public meetings were banned and local magistrates given more power to stop protestors from spreading their literature and arming themselves.*

(3 marks)

The Cato Street Conspiracy: *In 1820 a government spy discovered a plot to blow up leading members of the government, stage a coup and introduce a revolutionary form of government. The leading plotters were arrested at their house in London's Cato Street; their leader, Arthur Thistlewood, and several others were found guilty of treason and executed.*

(3 marks)

Total for exercise: 15 marks

Exercise 4.3

The explanation of why there was so much unrest in the first decades of the 19th century should demonstrate how the various factors are linked and comment on their relative importance. It should cover the following points:

- *Following the French Revolution, radical thinkers such as Thomas Paine called for parliamentary reform, including greater representation for ordinary people.*

- *Following the end of the Napoleonic War, there was less demand for uniforms and weapons. The textile, coal and iron industries suffered and many soldiers and sailors returned home to find there were no jobs.*

- *Industrial reform, such as the introduction of mechanical looms, meant that a smaller workforce was needed in some industries.*

- *Taxes introduced to pay Britain's war debts and protect the price of corn meant that the poor could not afford many ordinary goods, including bread.*

- *Many people felt that reforming how Parliament was elected would help solve these problems, by ensuring the election of MPs who were more sympathetic to the poor.*

(10 marks)

Exercise 4.4

Potwalloper boroughs: *At the beginning of the 19th century, the rules determining who could vote had not changed for centuries. In some boroughs, only a man who owned a house and had a fireplace upon which to boil a pot could vote; such boroughs were known as 'potwalloper' boroughs.*

(3 marks)

Pocket boroughs: *'Pocket boroughs' or 'rotten boroughs' were so called because, under the outdated rules, the vote was in someone's 'pocket' – so few people were eligible to vote that the owner of the land could decide who was elected.* (3 marks)

Earl Grey: *Earl Grey was Prime Minister of the Whig government. In the 1830s he heeded calls for a fairer system, putting forward a plan to redistribute parliamentary seats and introduce a uniform rule in all boroughs, giving the vote to everyone who owned a house worth £10. However, he was not interested in further reform, declaring himself against annual parliaments, universal suffrage and vote by secret ballot.* (3 marks)

The 3rd Reform Bill: *Grey's first two attempts at reform failed, but the third bill was pushed through the House of Commons and reached the House of Lords in May 1832. Grey asked King William IV to create enough new lords to overcome opposition to the bill, resigning when the king refused. However, Wellington was unable to form a Tory government, and Grey was recalled, with the king now willing to create the new lords. Meanwhile, pressure against the anti-reformers had convinced them to change their minds, and the bill became law on 7th June 1832.* (3 marks)

The Six Points: *The Six Points were the aims of the Chartist movement for political reform, as published in their first petition, in 1839. They demanded universal manhood suffrage, vote by secret ballot, annual parliaments, the abolition of property qualifications for MPs, a salary for MPs and equal electoral districts.* (3 marks)

William Lovett: *Lovett was one of the Chartist leaders, who acted as secretary to the Chartist Convention in 1839 and first published the Six Points. He supported 'moral force', or peaceful protest, rather than the 'physical force' backed by some other Chartists.* (3 marks)

Feargus O'Connor: *An Irish lawyer, O'Connor backed the 'physical force' trend in Chartism; he believed that when other forms of protest failed, change had to come through violence. He was elected an MP in 1847 and in 1848, he and several other Chartists carried a petition to Parliament, but Parliament refused to accept it. He died in 1855.* (3 marks)

The Newport Riot: *In 1839, a march of up to 5,000 Chartists entered Newport in South Wales to free fellow Chartists held in prison, carrying clubs, knives and other weapons. The Mayor of Newport brought 60 soldiers into the town and violence broke out. About 20 Chartists were killed and three soldiers injured. The riot gave the Whig government an excuse to crack down on Chartism, arresting the Chartist leaders, and sentencing three leaders of the Newport Rising to deportation to Australia.* (3 marks)

The Plug Riots: *In the early 1840s the 'Plug Riots', in which workers in the Midlands and north of England pulled the plugs out of steam engines in order to shut down their factories, were used as an excuse to arrest Chartist leaders, although it is not clear whether this was done in support of Chartism or was the result of local industrial disputes.* (3 marks)

Total for exercise: 27 marks

Exercise 4.5

1. *The writers of this source believe that Chartism will lead to revolution and loss of liberty.* (2 marks)

2. *This source suggests that Chartism will lead to a fairer society ('the repeal of bad laws and the making of good laws' and 'the abolition of ... abuses of the civil and criminal laws'), lower taxes, a 'liberal and general' education system and, as a result, less crime ('which would tend ... to diminish crime, but striking at its root').* (3 marks)

3. *Source C is in clear agreement with A concerning the negative effects of Chartism on Britain; it does not support B.* (7 marks)

4. A good answer will look at all the sources and conclude that all three sources are contemporary but reflect different viewpoints. It should cover the following points:

   - *Source A was written as part of an anti-Chartism campaign and is helpful in understanding the fears of those who opposed reform.*

   - *Source B is propaganda published by the Chartists. It was intended to convince the doubtful of the value of radical ideas, and so is helpful in understanding the Chartists' aims and beliefs.*

   - *Source C tells us the views of the cartoonish, George Cruikshank, regarding Chartism.* (8 marks)

Total for exercise: 20 marks

Exercise 4.6

The description of the events leading to the Reform Bill of 1832 should pick out the key events and recognise the importance of the events caused by the failure of the second bill in understanding the reasons for the eventual passage of the third bill.

- *The deaths of King George IV and Lord Liverpool and the collapse of the Tory government appeared to allow a chance for some political reform.*

- The new Whig government of Earl Grey put forward a plan to redistribute parliamentary seats and give the vote to every man who owned a house worth more than £10. However, Grey refused to consider further reform, declaring himself against annual parliaments, universal suffrage and vote by secret ballot.

- The first bill failed in 1831, when a majority in Parliament voted against it.

- A general election followed, with the Whigs campaigning on their reform plans. They won the election with a comfortable majority of 130.

- A number of political unions, such as the Birmingham Political Union (BPU), sprung up in support of reform. Radical reformers were distrustful of the unions, but most of the working classes were in support.

- The second bill was passed by the Whig majority in the House of Commons, but was defeated in the House of Lords by 41 votes.

- Rioting broke out in Nottingham, Derby and Bristol when the second bill failed. The BPU threatened to arm itself to put more pressure on politicians.

- The third bill was pushed through the House of Commons and reached the House of Lords in May 1832.

- Earl Grey asked King William IV to create enough new lords to overcome opposition, and resigned when the king refused.

- Wellington was unable to form a Tory government and Grey was recalled, with the king now willing to create the new lords.

- However, pressure against the anti-reformers had convinced many of them to change their minds, and the bill passed the House of Lords 106 to 22 and became law on 7th June 1932. (20 marks)

Exercise 4.7

The analysis of the success of the Chartist movement should identify and evaluate various factors. Modern historians continue to argue about the consequences of the Chartist movement; what is important here is not a 'right' answer but a clear comparison of the different factors and a clear and reasoned conclusion. The essay should cover the following points:

- The Chartist movement was a radical call for reform. It was never a single, united organisation. Its leaders included William Lovett, who supported 'moral force', or peaceful protest, and Feargus O'Connor, who backed 'physical force', believing that when other forms of protest failed, change had to come through violence.

- *Following the 3rd Reform Bill of 1832, there was no political will for further reform.*

- *Their first petition, published in 1839, called for the government to accept and act upon Six Points: universal manhood suffrage, vote by secret ballot, annual parliaments, the abolition of property qualification for MPs, a salary for MPs and equal electoral districts.*

- *The petition was ready to be presented to Parliament in May 1839, with 1.2 million signatures. However, it became apparent that Parliament had no intention of supporting any political reforms demanded by the Chartists. Middle class supporters of Chartism began to leave when they became alarmed by talk of physical force. The Newport Riot and Plug Riots gave the government the excuse to arrest Chartist leaders, although it is unclear whether the Plug Riots were part of the Chartist campaign.*

- *In 1848 another petition was produced and carried to Parliament on 10th April by O'Connor and several others. It was soon announced that of the nearly 6 million signatures, perhaps more than 3 million were not genuine, giving Parliament an excuse to refuse to accept the document. The Chartists saw 10th April as a success because they had peacefully presented the petition, but the government and the press viewed it as a disaster and a joke.*

- *Chartism then went into a slow decline until the last Chartist Convention met in 1858.*

- *With the exception of annual parliaments, all of the Chartists' Six Points were realised over time. For example, the secret ballot was introduced in 1872 and MPs began to be paid from 1911.*

(10 marks)

Chapter 5 The Agricultural and Industrial Revolutions

Exercise 5.1

Viscount 'Turnip' Townshend: *Townshend was associated with the new type of crop rotation system introduced from the Netherlands in the 1730s. This replaced the fallow year with a year growing turnips or clover, crops that used different nutrients from grain crops; turnips could be used to feed cattle, sheep and pigs, allowing them to be kept alive over the winter.*

(3 marks)

Robert Bakewell: *In Leicestershire in the 1760s, Robert Bakewell experimented with breeding sheep and cattle. He kept males and females apart, and chose animals with desired characteristics to breed, producing New Leicester sheep and a new breed of longhorn cows.*

(3 marks)

Arthur Young: *Young became a farm manager in Essex in 1767 and tried out new ideas, publishing their results in* A Course of Experimental Agriculture. *Although not successful himself, he inspired many other farmers to try new ideas and in 1793 he was made Secretary of the Board of Agriculture; he played a major role in producing agricultural surveys of English counties.*

(3 marks)

Jethro Tull: *In 1701, Tull invented the seed drill. This planted corn seed in neat rows, making it easier to cultivate.*

(3 marks)

Total for exercise: 12 marks

Exercise 5.2

Enclosure	was fencing in fields and common land to allow different farming techniques.
Crop rotation	was a method of farming land continually by changing what was grown on it.
The New Leicester sheep	was created by careful breeding by Robert Bakewell.
The Rotherham plough	was stronger and cheaper than its rivals when it was patented in 1730.
Steam engines	helped power many of the new machines that put farm labourers out of work.

The Board of Agriculture   was established to safeguard Britain's food supply during war.

Fallow land   was land that was allowed to 'rest' by not growing crops.

(7 marks)

Exercise 5.3

1. The description of the changes in agriculture in the 18th and 19th centuries should clearly organise the changes, show how they are linked and discuss how some developments had different impacts on different groups in Britain. It should cover the following points:

   - *A new crop rotation system meant that turnips could be used to keep cattle, sheep and pigs alive over the winter.*

   - *New technology such as the seed drill and Rotherham plough made crops easier to cultivate.*

   - *Robert Bakewell's breeding techniques improved the quality of livestock.*

   - *The new methods meant that land needed to be enclosed. Each farmer had his own land and common grazing land was lost. The new machinery meant that more land could be farmed by fewer people.*

   - *Some farmers became immediately prosperous but others did not thrive under the new system and sold up; they either worked for other farmers or moved to the city to get a job in a factory.* (20 marks)

2. The explanation of who prospered and who suffered because of the agricultural revolution should identify various factors and evaluate their importance. It should cover the following points:

   - *Following enclosure, some farmers immediately prospered, but others did not thrive. They could farm only their own land and could no longer graze pigs in the woods.*

   - *New technology meant that more land could be farmed by fewer people. Those who did not prosper found it difficult to find work for other farmers.*

   - *By the late 19th century, land was no longer jointly owned by villagers. Farmers now lived in farmhouses next to their fields, while the villages were occupied by the remaining farm labourers. Many families, who had worked the land for centuries, were forced to move to the towns and cities in search of work.* (10 marks)

Total for exercise: 30 marks

Exercise 5.4

Abraham Darby opens his works at Coalbrookdale	1708
Thomas Newcomen creates a usable steam engine	1712
John Kay invents the flying shuttle	1733
James Hargreaves creates the spinning jenny	1764
James Watt refines the steam engine	1765
Richard Arkwright invents the water frame	1769
Richard Arkwright creates the first factory at Cromford	1771
Boulton and Watt are established in Birmingham	1773
Henry Cort develops the puddling process	1784
The first iron bridge is built in Britain	1779 (10 marks)

Exercise 5.5

Blast furnaces: *Blast furnaces were used for smelting, in which iron ore and limestone were heated by burning charcoal; the limestone carried off impurities in the iron ore, forming slag and pig iron.* (3 marks)

Abraham Darby: *Abraham Darby founded an iron works in Coalbrookdale, Shropshire. He realised that most of the sulphur in coal could be driven off by partially burning the coal in a restricted space, producing coke, which could be used as a cheaper alternative to charcoal in the smelting process.* (3 marks)

Thomas Newcomen: *Newcomen produced the earliest working steam engine. It was huge and clumsy and used up great amounts of coal; poor transportation meant that anyone wanting to use a Newcomen engine had to construct it on site, following Newcomen's instructions and having the parts made locally. However, it became a tried and trusted technology, and it was a model Newcomen engine that inspired James Watt to try to harness the power of steam effectively.* (3 marks)

Puddling: *Henry Cort patented the puddling process in 1784. Iron was melted in a separate chamber, so that it didn't come into contact with coal, then stirred to allow carbon in the iron to combine with the oxen and drift away. More wrought iron could now be produced and its price fell; by the mid 19th century it was the material of choice for manufacturing.* (3 marks)

Flying shuttle: *The flying shuttle was invented in 1733 by John Kay. Previously weavers had to pass the thread back and forth across the loom by hand. Kay's device allowed the thread, on a shuttle, to be mechanically sent back and forth. This greatly sped up the weaving, and Kay was attacked on several occasions by textile workers who feared for their jobs.* (3 marks)

James Hargreaves: *A weaver, in 1764 Hargreaves invented the spinning jenny. A whole line of spindles, each holding one thread, could now be spun using one wheel. His machines were smashed by fearful workers.* (3 marks)

Richard Arkwright: *In 1769 Arkwright invented the water frame. This improved on the spinning jenny in several ways. It was so large it could not be powered by hand, but needed a larger source of power. At first he tried horses, then turned to a waterwheel, going on to build a number of water-powered cotton mills.* (3 marks)

Cromford: *Arkwright built his first cotton mill at Cromford, Derbyshire, in 1771. Situated in a valley, Cromford had a stream that did not freeze in winter and which flowed strongly even in dry summer. For the first time, the whole industrial process was under one roof, powered and using cheap labour, making Cromford the first real factory in Britain. Arkwright also built homes for his workers, a school, a chapel and an inn.* (3 marks)

James Watt: *Born in 1736, Watt worked as an apprentice instrument maker before establishing his own business in Scotland in 1756. He became interested in the idea of harnessing the power of steam and in 1765 realised that the key was to use a separate chamber to condense the steam and create a vacuum. By the time he retired in 1800, Watt had devised several other improvements to steam engines, and he and his business partner Matthew Boulton had produced 500 working engines. Watt died in 1819.* (3 marks)

Matthew Boulton: *Matthew Boulton and James Watt met in Birmingham, where Boulton had a metalworks. In 1773 he convinced Watt to move to Birmingham. They became business partners, and Boulton helped Watt create a workable steam engine, organising a means of producing an accurately made, steam-tight working cylinder, using a new boring mill for making cannon.* (3 marks)

The Lunar Society: *The Lunar Society was a group of forward-thinking men who met in Birmingham on the Sunday or Monday closest to the full moon. Watt was introduced to the group by Boulton, and the society helped Watt become a success as an engineer and an industrialist.* (3 marks)

John Wilkinson: *The brother-in-law of Lunar Society member Joseph Priestley, John Wilkinson had created a new boring mill for making cannon. This was adapted to produce the accurately made, steam-tight working cylinders needed to make Watt's steam engine work.*

(3 marks)

Total for exercise: 36 marks

Exercise 5.6

Both of these essays should show a clear chronological structure and make use of a good deal of accurate information.

(a) A good description of the life and career of an important figure in the Industrial Revolution will clearly link the chosen figure to the development of one or, in the case of Wilkinson, more than one industry at the time.   (20 marks)

(b) A good description of the changes that occurred in one industry during this period will make clear causal connections, showing how and why the chosen industry developed over time.   (20 marks)

Exercise 5.7

Both of these essays require an analytical approach.

(a) The explanation of the consequences to a particular industry of the inventions and actions of one important person could include an argument that one consequence is more important that the others, explaining this and linking the other consequences identified to the most important result.   (10 marks)

(b) The explanation of the reasons why major changes occurred in a particular industry could consider various different kinds of causes, for example economic, demographic and scientific.   (10 marks)

Chapter 6 The transportation revolution

Exercise 6.1

Travelling around England in the 18th century **Arthur Young** wrote of the **sorry** state of the roads. This began to improve with Parliament setting up **turnpike trusts**. **Tollgates** were set up to collect the turnpike fees. Better road surfaces and construction by road builders such as **John Metcalf** and **Thomas Telford** greatly improved the roads but it was **John McAdam** who produced the cheapest method, called a **macadam** surface. Improved roads led to the golden age of the **stagecoaches**. Heavier goods could travel by **stagewagon**. (10 marks)

Exercise 6.2

Arthur Young: *Young was a commentator on the state of the roads in Britain in the 18th century.* (3 marks)

Turnpikes: *In order to improve the roads, from the late 17th century Parliament passed private acts giving groups of local landowners and merchants the right to set up turnpike trusts. Each trust was responsible for repairing and maintaining a particular stretch of road and in exchange could charge a toll from road users.* (3 marks)

Stagecoaches: *Stagecoaches travelled in stages, stopping at inns to change teams of horses, hence the name. This type of travel became successful as a result of improvements to the roads made by turnpike trusts.* (3 marks)

John McAdam: *McAdam came up with a cheap and popular method of building roads. A platform of medium stones was covered with a shallow layer of small granite chips. The weight of carts, wagons and coaches using this surface pressed it down into what became known as a 'macadam' surface.* (3 marks)

The Rebecca riots: *In a time of poor harvests and high taxes, the poor objected to the high toll charges. In South Wales between 1839 and 1844, there were a series of attacks upon tollgates by men dressed as women, which became known as the Rebecca riots.* (3 marks)

Total for exercise: 15 marks

Exercise 6.3

The third Duke of Bridgewater	was a pioneer in the building of the first canals.
John Gilbert	was the Duke of Bridgewater's estate agent who played a key role in building his canal.
James Brindley	was a self-taught engineer who built the Barton Aqueduct.
Puddling	was James Brindley's solution to sealing the bed of a canal.
Josiah Wedgwood	wanted a way to move his pottery, leading to the construction of the Trent and Mersey Canal.
Canal mania	was the result of too many people trying to make money investing in canals.
Thomas Telford	built the aqueduct at Pontcysyllte, roads in the Highlands and the Holyhead road, among other projects.
Isambard Kingdom Brunel	designed a bridge across the Avon Gorge that was rejected by Thomas Telford but was the design chosen.
Navvy	was shortened from 'navigators' and was the name given to the men who dug the canals.

(10 marks)

Exercise 6.4

The third Duke of Bridgewater: *Bridgewater was a key pioneer in the development of the canal system in Britain. He wanted to find a better market for the coal mined on his property and, with his estate agent John Gilbert, came up with the idea of a cross-country canal to Salford, Manchester. James Brindley was chief engineer on the project.* (3 marks)

James Brindley: *A millwright, building waterways and improving the rivers that fed them, Brindley had gained skills in digging waterways and was appointed chief engineer on the building of the Bridgewater Canal. This included the remarkable Barton Aqueduct over the River Irwell, which was 60m long, with three brick arches and 12m above the river at its highest point. However, Brindley's design for canal locks would have been a disaster if the duke had not stepped in and insisted on using known designs. Brindley also came up with the 'puddling' technique for sealing the bed of a canal, using several layers of a mixture of clay, sand and water.* (3 marks)

Navvies: *The workmen who built canals were known as 'navigators', or 'navvies' for short. They dug out the canals, cutting through hills and making tunnels, and sealed the canal beds using the puddling technique. Navvies lived in makeshift huts, drank hard and could be unruly.*

(3 marks)

Canal mania: *During the early 1790s, a number of new canals were built. These brought their owners huge sums of money in tolls and other charges. As a result, the demand for Acts of Parliament to build new canals exploded. However, in the mid 1790s, the war against revolutionary France and a financial crisis brought the mania to an abrupt halt, and many of the planned canals were never built; many that were never made a profit.*   (3 marks)

The aqueduct at Pontcysyllte: *Thomas Telford built the Pontcysyllte Aqueduct as part of the Ellesmere Canal. It stretched for 300m at a height of 40m. The water flowed through a cast iron trough set upon stone piers, demonstrating Telford's mastery of the use of iron.*

(3 marks)

The Holyhead road: *Thomas Telford was involved in the major project to improve the road between Holyhead in Wales and London. The new road cut the journey, which had been slow, uncomfortable and dangerous, by nine hours. Telford insisted on creating a solid road foundation, and also designed and built magnificent suspension bridges at the Menai Strait and Conwy; the bridges challenged his engineering abilities as they needed to withstand high winds.*

(3 marks)

Total for exercise: 18 marks

Exercise 6.5

Richard Trevithick creates the first successful steam locomotive	1804
Trevithick's *Catch-Me-Who-Can* is shown in London	1808
George Stephenson builds the *Blucher*	1814
Opening of the Stockton and Darlington Railway	1825
Rainhill Locomotive trials	1829
Opening of the Liverpool and Manchester Railway	1830
Isambard Kingdom Brunel begins work on the Great Western Railway	1835
Queen Victoria takes her first trip on the railways	1842
George Hudson, the Railway King, is found to be a fraud	1847
All of Britain is required to use the standard, or railway, time	1880

(10 marks)

Exercise 6.6

Richard Trevithick: *Trevithick was a Cornish mining engineer who experimented with using steam under pressure to create power, and in 1802 patented a new engine that used super-heated steam working at six or seven times the pressure of the surrounding atmosphere. In 1804 he developed the first steam engine light enough to be mounted on a cart to propel itself. However, he could not manage money and died a poor man in 1833.* (3 marks)

The *Blucher*: The Blucher *was George Stephenson's first attempt to build a steam locomotive for the Killingworth Colliery. It could pull 30 tonnes of weight up a hill at 4 miles an hour. It was the first engine to use flanged wheels to hold it on to the rails and rely on friction between wheels and track to make it move.* (3 marks)

The Stockton and Darlington Railway: *The Stockton and Darlington Railway ran for 27 miles, linking a number of collieries to the River Tees. Initially the wagons were to be drawn by horses but, following his success with the Blucher, George Stephenson was hired to be chief engineer and steam locomotives were used. The railway's success was the making of Stephenson and the gauge used for the rails is still used in railways all over the world today.* (3 marks)

The Rainhill trials: *In October 1829 a competition was held at Rainhill near Liverpool to decide how to power the Liverpool and Manchester Railway. The winning engine, George and Robert Stephenson's Rocket, used the new idea of a multi-tube boiler that increased the amount of steam the engine could produce and not only pulled the required weight for the necessary distance but at times managed to reach the unheard for speed of 30 miles per hour. It convinced the directors of the railway that steam locomotives were the way forward.* (3 marks)

George Hudson: *Known as the 'Railway King', Hudson built on an initial investment in a railway to become Chairman of the York and Midland Railway and eventually gained control of 1,000 miles of railway. Greatly admired, he was Mayor of York and an MP, but he was cheating the system, using money he gained from one group of shareholders to pay the dividend to other shareholders; when he was found out in 1847 the whole scheme collapsed, bringing railway mania to an end.* (3 marks)

The Great Western Railway: *Linking Bristol to London, the Great Western Railway was the work of Isambard Kingdom Brunel. The gauge of the line was 213cm, not 143.5cm as with the other main lines, allowing faster, smoother travel and more comfortable carriages. In 1842, Queen Victoria made her first-ever railway trip on the GWR, with Brunel helping to drive the engine.* (3 marks)

SS Great Eastern: *The SS Great Eastern was Brunel's last big project. The ship was launched successfully only after several very public false starts and she suffered an explosion during her first voyage. News of this was probably the last straw for Brunel, whose health had been failing for some time and who collapsed with a stroke on 5th September 1859, dying 10 days later.*

(3 marks)

Total for exercise: 24 marks

Exercise 6.7

Both of these essays should show a clear chronological narrative and make links between the different events described.

(a) A good description of the life of one of the key figures in the transportation revolution will clearly place the chosen figure in the wider developments of the transportation revolution.

(20 marks)

(b) A good description of a major development or event in the transportation revolution will show both how the development or event was caused by the revolution and how it affected the revolution.

(20 marks)

Exercise 6.8

Both of these essays require an analytical approach and should do more than simply list the winners and losers or reasons for the demand for roads, canals or railways.

(a) The explanation of who benefited and who suffered because of the development of the railways could establish whether more people benefited than suffered.

(10 marks)

(b) The explanation of the reasons why the roads, canals or railways developed should either categorise the reasons identified as economic, political and so on, or argue for one reason as the most important.

(10 marks)

Exercise 6.9

1. *Source A claims that George Stephenson was important because his contribution to the railway network (as 'Father of Railways') changed Britain for the better ('left the world a totally different place').* (2 marks)

2. *The writer of Source B points out that Stephenson came from a humble ('modest working-class') background and was skilled ('possessed considerable skills in both civil and mechanical engineering') but considers him a 'bully' who 'fawned' on greater men.* (3 marks)

3. *Source C shows Stephenson surrounded by his family and his inventions, and therefore agrees with Source A in showing how important he was. However, it does not agree with Source B, which questions Stephenson's role and points out his 'bad' side.* (7 marks)

4. A good answer will look at all the sources and refer to both their content and provenance. It should cover the following points:

   - *Source A is taken from a modern biography of Stephenson and is therefore a useful assessment of his achievements and how the birth of the railways changed Britain.*

   - *Source B is also taken from a modern biography of Stephenson. It concentrates on his character and tells us little about his role in the birth of the railways.*

   - *Source C is a painting done in the Victorian period, so probably contemporary, but shows people and objects that would never have been together. It is useful in that it shows how some Victorians saw Stephenson as a hero.* (8 marks)

   Total for exercise: 20 marks

Chapter 7 Social and industrial reform

Exercise 7.1

Granville Sharp saves Jonathan Strong from being resold into slavery	1767
James Somerset is freed	1772
The *Zong* case is taken to trial	1783
Formation of the Society for the Abolition of the Slave Trade	1787
Passage of the Dolben Act	1788
Collapse of anti-slave trade reform because of the outbreak of the French Revolution	1793
Foreign Slave Trade Act is passed	1806
Act passed in Parliament to abolish the trade in slaves	1807
Formation of the Society for the Mitigation and Gradual Abolition of Slavery	1823
Slavery Abolition Act	1833

(10 marks)

Exercise 7.2

Triangular trade: *The triangular trade was the movement of British ships from Britain to Africa, carrying cargos such as cloth to be traded for ivory, slaves and other cargo, then from Africa to the Americas and the West Indies to sell the slaves, and then back to Britain with another cargo, such as sugar or raw cotton.* (3 marks)

The middle passage: *The second leg of the triangular trade, from Africa to the Americas and the West Indies, was known as 'the middle passage'. The ships were often filled as full as possible with profitable slaves, risking the outbreak of disease. The conditions the slaves were kept in were cramped, hot and filthy.* (3 marks)

Granville Sharp: *Talented and eccentric, Sharp was the first non-Quaker to protest against slavery. He became involved when he met Jonathan Strong, who had been beaten until he was nearly blind and then abandoned on the streets of London by his owner. Sharp and his brother helped Strong and later prevented him from being returned to his old master. In 1772 Sharp prevented another slave, James Somerset, from being sent to Jamaica against his will. Sharp was also a founding member of the Society for the Abolition of the Slave Trade.* (3 marks)

James Somerset: *Somerset was brought to Britain as a slave from the colony of Virginia, but escaped his master. When he was recaptured, his owner arranged for him to be sent to Jamaica, but Somerset appealed to law. The final judgement ruled that Somerset could not be forced to go to another country by his master, but stopped short of setting slaves free in Britain. Granville Sharp was involved in the case and it aroused a lot of public interest.*

(3 marks)

Thomas Clarkson: *Clarkson had meant to join the church but felt the call to focus on the great evil of slavery. He travelled the country collecting accounts of the slave trade, finding witnesses and evidence of the vile nature of the business. In 1787 he enlisted the support of William Wilberforce.* (3 marks)

William Wilberforce: *Wilberforce was a young MP from Hull, and a good friend of the Prime Minister, William Pitt. An Evangelical member of the Church of England, Wilberforce agreed to speak against slavery in Parliament. In 1789 and 1791 he presented a Bill to outlaw the slave trade, but each time it failed to become law. However, in 1806 he presented the successful Foreign Slave Trade Act and in 1807 a Bill completely banning the British slave trade was signed into law. Wilberforce died one month before slavery was finally abolished, with the passing of the Slavery Abolition Act, in 1833.* (3 marks)

Olaudah Equiano: *In 1789, former slave Olaudah Equiano published his autobiography, which included accounts of his kidnapping, aged 12, and his experiences on board a slave ship. He travelled Great Britain for five years selling his book and proving that Africans were not the backward and primitive people that many British people had thought.* (3 marks)

James Stephen: *An expert on maritime law who had lived in the West Indies and seen the evils of slavery first hand, Stephen spotted a way to strike at the slave trade that neither slave traders nor West Indian planters could protest about. The Foreign Slave Trade Act, which passed through Parliament in 1806, banned British ships and sailors from being involved in trading slaves with any French colonies or with any of France's allies, such as Spain. This made the slave trade much less profitable for Britain, but objections would be seen as unpatriotic.*

(3 marks)

Sir Thomas Buxton: *The Quaker Sir Thomas Buxton took over from Wilberforce as spokesman for the anti-slavery movement in Parliament in the early 1820s. He described the slave trade as 'repugnant'.* (3 marks)

Elizabeth Heyrick: *The widow of a Quaker army officer, Elizabeth Heyrick was one of the leaders of the women's groups, formed in the 1820s, that demanded immediate action to end the slave trade. She believed that earlier calls for gradual emancipation had damaged the campaign.* (3 marks)

Agency Anti-Slavery Committee: *The Agency Anti-Slavery Committee was created by some of the more radical abolitionists, led by men like George Stephen, son of James. In the early 1830s, they sent out professional speakers to raise public support.* (3 marks)

Emancipation Act of 1834: *In the early 1830s, the government became concerned about slave revolts and slavery officially ended in British colonies on 1st August 1834, with the passing of the Emancipation Act. In order to gain support, the Bill stated that only slave children six years old and under would be freed immediately, while the rest would have to spend between four and six years working as apprentices on low wages for their former owners first; slave owners were also compensated for the loss of their 'property'. However, many apprentices were treated by their masters as if they were still slaves, and the abolitionists reassembled to demand the end of the apprenticeship system, achieving success in 1838.* (3 marks)

Total for exercise: 36 marks

Exercise 7.3

Because of the **Industrial** Revolution there was an **increase** in the number of people being sent to **prison** in the early 19th century. **Quaker** women like Elizabeth Fry had a tradition of helping the poor. When **Stephen Grellet** told Elizabeth about the conditions in **Newgate** Prison she visited immediately, taking **clothing** and **straw**. When she returned **four** years later she organised a **school** for the children and materials so that the women prisoners could **sew** or **knit**. What Elizabeth Fry managed to achieve in reforming prisons included stopping the practice of **whipping** prisoners and helping to create **committees** throughout Europe to help bring reform. (15 marks)

Exercise 7.4

Outdoor relief: *Until 1834, each parish looked after their own poor using money from the Poor Rate, a tax paid by all property owners. Outdoor relief was money given to the poor, to help large families trying to survive on low wages remain in their own homes.* (3 marks)

Jeremy Bentham: *The philosopher Jeremy Bentham believed that government should be as efficient and accountable as possible, and that people were motivated to avoid pain and seek pleasure. He and his followers believed in 'the greatest happiness of the greatest number'. His influence helped persuade the Whig government to set up the Royal Commission on the Poor Laws in 1832, which led to the New Poor Law of 1834.* (3 marks)

Workhouses: *Workhouses were special buildings where the poor people of a parish could be housed in return for doing work for the parish; this was known as 'indoor relief'. Under the*

New Poor Law of 1834, control of the workhouses was centralised so that the level of relief would be the same for everyone. Conditions within the workhouses were intended to encourage the poor to find work as soon as possible and leave: families were split up and men and women housed separately; the work was boring and sometimes pointless, and inmates wore ugly uniforms as if they were in prison; food was poor and often limited.

(3 marks)

The Poor Law Board: In 1847, following a number of scandals in which workhouse managers stole from the funds given to them, and provided the poor in their care with starvation rations and rags to wear, the Poor Law Commission was replaced by the Poor Law Board. The new board was responsible to a government minister and Parliament.   (3 marks)

Edwin Chadwick: A follower of Bentham, Chadwick was a key member of the Commission on the Poor Laws and chair of the Royal Commission set up in 1833 to re-examine working conditions in the cotton industry. This commission ignored the moral and religious concerns of the Evangelicals but concluded that the working hours of children should be restricted. He objected to Elizabeth Fry's work in prisons, complaining that she was turning them into comfortable places that would attract the unworthy poor, but he played a leading role in many reforms of the period.   (3 marks)

Ten Hours Movement: The Ten Hours Movement developed in the 1830s with the aim of restricting the working day for children to ten hours a day. Their voice in Parliament, Michael Sadler, chaired a Select Committee that produced a very critical report of conditions in the mills and attempted to push a Bill through Parliament, but in the elections after the 1832 Reform Act Sadler was not re-elected. However, Anthony Ashley Cooper (later Lord Shaftesbury), resubmitted the Bill and reform, although slow, followed.   (3 marks)

Factory Act of 1833: The Factory Act of 1833 restricted the number of hours children could work per day, according to age, and required them to be given two hours of education a day. However, it failed to have much impact because many parents wanted and needed the income from their children and mill owners did their best to beat the new restrictions. In addition, until new laws over birth registration came into force in the 1840s, it was very hard to determine a child's true age.   (3 marks)

Total for exercise: 21 marks

Exercise 7.5

1. *Gillray shows the slave being held down in a boiling vat of cane sugar with the end of a whip. This clearly shows that Gillary considered slave owners to be guilty of cruelty to their slaves.*
   (2 marks)

2. *The Earl of Abingdon identifies the 'French principles' of 'insubordination, anarchy, confusion, murder, havock, devastation and ruin' and implies that these will be the result of the abolition of slavery.*
   (3 marks)

3. *Source C shows that Gillray thinks supporting abolition is wrong and agrees with Source B, which claims that abolition would bring anarchy. Source C, even though drawn by the same artist, does not agree with Source A, as A shows the extreme cruelty of slavery and is against it.*
   (7 marks)

4. A good answer will look at all the sources and refer to both their content and provenance. It should cover the following points:

   - *All of these sources have their use for a historian.*

   - *Sources A and C are by the same contemporary artist and reflect popular opinion at the time, although they could also be considered propaganda both for and against slavery.*

   - *Source B shows clearly how many politicians of the time viewed abolition and is useful in that way, but it does not necessarily reflect more popular opinion.*
   (8 marks)

   Total for exercise: 20 marks

Exercise 7.6

Both of these essays should show a clear chronological narrative and make links between the different events described.

(a) A good description of the attempts of a movement for social reform to achieve its aims will show the different approaches used and point out key individuals and events.
   (20 marks)

(b) A good description of the role of an important figure within a movement for social reform will clearly place the chosen figure in the reform movement and examine his or her motivation and actions.
   (20 marks)

Exercise 7.7

Both of these essays require an analytical approach and should do more than simply list the winners and losers or simply state whether a figure was successful.

(a) The explanation of the consequences of a movement for social reform on the lives of the people of Britain should either categorise the reasons identified as economic, political and so on, or argue for one reason as the most important; alternatively, it could evaluate who benefited and who did not. (10 marks)

(b) The explanation of how successful an important figure within a movement for social reform was in achieving his or her aims should argue in what ways he or she was successful, and in what ways he or she was not successful, before reaching an overall conclusion. (10 marks)

Chapter 8 A decade of success: the Great Exhibition and the Crimean War

Exercise 8.1

The man who first came up with the idea of a Great Exhibition was	Henry Cole.
The Natural History Museum	was one of the results of the Great Exhibition.
The eventual plan for the Exhibition's building was by	Joseph Paxton.
Prince Albert was	a chief organiser of the Exhibition.
Special excursions for the Great Exhibition	were set up by the railway companies.
The magazine *Punch*	coined the name Crystal Palace.
On the opening day many people	feared there would be riots and the building would collapse.
Queen Victoria	was a frequent visitor to the Great Exhibition.

(8 marks)

Exercise 8.2

Joseph Paxton: *Paxton was a garden architect who, by chance, sat next to MP John Ellis at a business meeting. Paxton doodled an idea for a structure on his blotter sheet. Ellis liked it and showed it to Henry Cole, who got it approved instead of the winning entry.* (3 marks)

Crystal Palace: *The building that housed the Great Exhibition stretched 563m from east to west and was 139m wide. At its highest point it was 32m from the ground and a row of elm trees were left standing inside it. The structure of glass and iron was largely made elsewhere and only assembled at the site. It was given the name 'Crystal Palace' by the magazine* Punch. (3 marks)

Great Exhibition of 1851: *The Great Exhibition was intended to display Britain's technological and commercial might. Half of the space was reserved for Great Britain and its colonies, and the other half offered to other countries. The exhibits included steam engines, textiles, statues, ceramics, teapots, stuffed animals and guns.*

Shilling day entry: *The usual entry price for the Exhibition was £3, but on some days it was dropped to one shilling, to allow poorer people to visit the Exhibition. Clergymen, landlords, factory owners and others paid for agricultural labourers, factory workers, clerks and so on, for whom one shilling was still too expensive, to attend. It was unusual for the different social classes at Britain to attend the same event in this way.* (3 marks)

Results of the Great Exhibition: *As well as demonstrating the might and triumphs of Britain to both the world and its own citizens, the Great Exhibition showed the upper and middle classes that the working classes could behave in an orderly fashion. Railway companies began to run excursion trains to other destinations. The profits of the Exhibition were used to build places devoted to public learning and entertainment, including the Royal Albert Hall and the Science, Natural History, and Victoria and Albert Museums.* (3 marks)

Total for exercise: 12 marks

Exercise 8.3

(a) A good description of the Great Exhibition of 1851 will present a good selection of information explaining why the event was planned and describing the building, its contents and how people visited the exhibition. The best answers will also include some of the controversy surrounding the Exhibition and/or some of the social tensions involved. It should cover the following points:

- *The Great Exhibition was intended to demonstrate Britain's technological and commercial might.*

- *Crystal Palace was built in Hyde Park, to Joseph Paxton's design. A gigantic greenhouse made of glass and iron, it provided 91,975 m² of exhibition space.*

- *The exhibits from Britain, its colonies and other countries around the world included steam engines, textiles, stuffed animals and many other items.*

- *People of all classes visited the Exhibition. The price was dropped to one shilling on certain days to allow the poorer people to attend; benefactors paid for those for whom this was still too expensive. Railway companies ran special excursion trains from all over the country.*

- *Thousands of policemen and regiments of cavalry were at the ready at the grand opening on 1st May 1851, but the expected trouble did not materialise.*

- *The upper and middle classes were surprised at the orderly behaviour of the working classes.*

- *Queen Victoria made a point of attending on several one shilling days in order to see and be seen by her middle and working class subjects.* (20 marks)

(b) A good explanation of how the Great Exhibition affected the lives of the people of Britain will show judgement, possibly by comparing and contrasting the consequences of the Exhibition; another approach could be to examine the consequences by category, such as economic, social, educational, etc. It should cover the following points:

- *The Great Exhibition demonstrated the might and triumphs of Britain to both the world and its own citizens.*

- *It showed the upper and middle classes that the working classes could behave in an orderly fashion.*

- *Railway companies began to run excursion trains to other destinations.*

- *The profits of the Exhibition were used to build places devoted to public learning and entertainment, including the Royal Albert Hall and the Science, Natural History and Victoria and Albert Museums.*

(10 marks)

Total for exercise: 30 marks

Exercise 8.4

The Crimean War started in the year **1854**. It was caused by the slow collapse of the **Ottoman Empire** and **Russia's** plan to divide it up. **France** and **Britain** decided to oppose this, leading to war. The British army was **small, poorly led** and **badly equipped** for the war. Poor leadership was especially shown at the Battle of **Balaklava** with the Charge of the **Light Brigade**. (10 marks)

Exercise 8.5

The importance of Istanbul: *Britain and France were worried that if the Russians seized Istanbul the Tsar would become too powerful and might dominate the Mediterranean.*

(3 marks)

The Battle of Balaklava: *The most famous battle of the war took place at Balaklava, where a series of redoubts or fortifications which overlooked the British supply base were seized from the Turks by the Russians. British troops blocked the Russian advance, but then the Light Cavalry Brigade charged and was overwhelmed by the force of Russian guns and infantry, and forced to retreat. The Charge of the Light Brigade is remembered as both an infamous mistake and a measure of British bravery.*

(3 marks)

William Howard Russell: *Russell was a journalist for the* Times *who reported on the Crimean War from the front lines, using the new technologies of the telegraph and* steamships. This was the first time the British public had been able to follow the progress of a war closely; reports of the terrible conditions for the sick and wounded led Mary Seacole and Florence Nightingale to go to the Crimea to nurse the man. (3 marks)

The British Hotel: When Mary Seacole, the daughter of a white Scottish officer and a former slave in Jamaica, heard that some of the British regiments she had known in Jamaica had been sent to the Crimea, she travelled to Britain to offer her services as a nurse. When she was turned down, at least in part because she was mixed race, she went into partnership with a Mr Day to establish a post close to the front line to provide meals, medical care and home comforts to the soldiers; this became known as 'the British Hotel'. (3 marks)

Scutari: In 1854, Florence Nightingale and a party of 38 nurses arrived at the British army hospital in Scutari to help nurse the sick and wounded soldiers of the Crimean War. The hospital was small, poorly organised and built over a refuse dump. Despite the disapproval of the military medical staff, who felt that the care of soldiers was an unsuitable task for young ladies, Nightingale worked to improve conditions and became famous for her kindness and patience. (3 marks)

Sidney Herbert: Herbert was the Secretary of State for War who invited Florence Nightingale to take a party of nurses to the Crimea. Nightingale remained in contact with Herbert, describing to him both the conditions she found and her attempts to improve matters.
(3 marks)

'The Lady with the Lamp': Florence Nightingale became known as 'the Lady with the Lamp' because before going to bed at night she would walk the dark hospital with a lamp, stopping to make sure that everything was in order and that nobody needed anything. In Britain she was seen as a heroine and when she returned after the war she continued to push for reform. Her belief that disease was spread by bad air was mistaken, and she did not support the idea of women becoming doctors, but she did much to improve the education and status of nurses, and helped to transform the way the British Army dealt with its sick and wounded.
(3 marks)

Total for exercise: 21 marks

Exercise 8.6

1. *The picture shows the charge coming under heavy fire and a number of men and horses falling, so it does not show the charge as a success although the men are still charging.*

    (2 marks)

2. *Tennyson says that in ordering the charge, 'Some one had blunder'd', and goes on to state that the soldiers had no choice but to 'do and die', indicating that the charge was a mistake that led to the deaths of many in the Light Brigade.* (3 marks)

3. *Source C talks about 'bad Generalship', supporting Source B's claim that 'Some one had blunder'd'. However, it does not support Source A in that it does not mention the Light Brigade reaching the Russian guns.* (7 marks)

4. A good answer will look at all the sources and refer to both their content and, in particular, their provenance. It should cover the following points:

    - *Source A, which was published in a newspaper, and source B, a published poem, were for mass consumption and would therefore be very influential in terms of public perception of the event, although they are not very accurate.*

    - *Source C is an account by a participant in the charge, and is therefore more accurate, but since it was a private letter it would not have been read by many people at the time.*

        (8 marks)

    Total for exercise: 20 marks

Exercise 8.7

1. Both of these essays should show a clear chronological narrative and link the chosen individual to the key events of the movement for reform.

    (a) A good description of the role of an important figure who tried to reform social conditions in this period should link the chosen individual to specific reforms and describe his or her role in attempting to carry them out.

        (20 marks)

    (b) A good description of the life of a well-known woman during this period should point out the events that could be considered the most important in shaping the chosen woman's life. (20 marks)

2. Both of these essays require an analytical approach and should either create an argument or show judgement by categorising types of factors.

(a) The explanation of why a well-known woman of this time period is remembered today should state the main reason why the chosen woman is known and then explain why this is, making links to other reasons.

(10 marks)

(b) The explanation of why an important figure tried to reform social conditions during this time should either state and explain the main reason, making links to other reasons, or categorise several different factors as economic, political, religious, and so on.

(10 marks)

Total for exercise: 60 marks

Chapter 9 Queen Victoria, government and politics

Exercise 9.1

Victoria was born in **1819** to the Duke and Duchess of **Kent** and was the only living grandchild of George III. Her widowed mother and Sir **John Conroy** kept tight control of her as she grew up. Princess Victoria proved to be good at languages such as **German, Italian** and **French**. She was **18** years old when she became queen with the death of her uncle King **William IV** in the year **1837**. (10 marks)

Exercise 9.2

Lord Melbourne: *Melbourne was the Whig Prime Minister when Victoria became queen. He took her under his wing and helped her adjust to her new position.* (3 marks)

Prince Albert of Saxe-Coburg: *Prince Albert was Victoria's husband and consort. At first some in Britain were unhappy that their young queen had married a foreign prince, but eventually he overcame their suspicion. He helped his wife come to terms with working with politicians she did not like, and took over the management of the royal household and estates. Albert died in 1861; Victoria mourned him for the rest of her life.* (3 marks)

Osborne House: *Victoria and Albert spent time at Osborne House, on the Isle of Wight, with their nine children. There, and at Balmoral in Scotland, Albert helped create places where they could enjoy something resembling normal family life.* (3 marks)

The Bedchamber Crisis: *In 1939 Lord Melbourne lost a key vote in Parliament and resigned, and the Tory Sir Robert Peel was asked to take over. Victoria found Peel difficult to work with and refused his request that some of Melbourne's friends in the royal household be replaced with her own supporters. Victoria thought that the royal household was her business, despite that fact that some of the positions had political aspects. She backed down after the 1841 general election, which Peel won handsomely.* (3 marks)

Total for exercise: 12 marks

Exercise 9.3

Victoria became queen	1837
Marriage of Queen Victoria to Prince Albert	1840
Robert Peel became Prime Minister with a Tory majority	1841
Mines Act which stops women and children from working underground	1842
Repeal of the Corn Laws	1846
Gladstone and Disraeli were both Prime Ministers in this year	1868
Elementary Education Act requires all children from the age of five to attend school	1870
Ballot Act allowed secret ballot in elections	1872
Disraeli becomes Prime Minister after defeat of Gladstone and the Liberals	1874
The Artisans' Dwelling Act tries to deal with slums	1875
Britain buys 44% share in the Suez Canal	1875
Disraeli lost election as Prime Minister for the last time	1880
Queen Victoria's Golden Jubilee	1887
Death of Queen Victoria	1901

(14 marks)

Exercise 9.4

The Corn Laws: Set up to protect the price of corn grown by British farmers at the end of the Napoleonic War in 1815, the Corn Laws were repealed in 1815. The Tory Prime Minister, Sir Robert Peel, believed that they stood in the way of free trade and argued that, by keeping the price of bread high, they caused hardship and starvation among the urban poor. Most Tories supported the Corn Laws because they protected the price of crops grown on their land, and the act repealing the laws passed only because the Whigs supported it.

(3 marks)

The Peelites: Following the repeal of the Corn Laws, the Tory party was split between the Peelites, who supported Peel, and the Protectionists, who did not.

(3 marks)

Elementary Education Act of 1870: *The Elementary Education Act established a system of state-run elementary schools, or 'board' schools, which were set up alongside the existing church schools. Following the act, all British children from the age of five were required to attend school until at least 11.* (3 marks)

Ballot Act of 1872: *Passed during Gladstone's first term as Prime Minister, the Ballot Act finally put in place one of the six Chartist points, that of a secret ballot.* (3 marks)

Factory Acts of 1874, 1878: *The two Factory Acts of 1874 and 1878 reduced working hours to ten per day and brought both factories and workshops under government inspection.* (3 marks)

Home Rule: *In his third term as Prime Minister, Gladstone decided that the only way to control growing unrest in Ireland was to grant it a limited amount of independence, known as Home Rule. An explosive issue, Home Rule caused a storm within Gladstone's own party and a large group of Liberals broke away to join the Conservatives, who were steadfast against Home Rule.* (3 marks)

Suez Canal: *In 1875, Disraeli grabbed the opportunity to buy a 44% share in the Suez Canal, an important link between Britain and its Asian empire, and in particular India.* (3 marks)

Empress of India: *Queen Victoria was given the title Empress of India by Disraeli's government. This strengthened ties with the part of the Empire that Disraeli referred to as the 'jewel in the crown' of Britain and gained favour with the queen.* (3 marks)

The Eastern Question: *The Eastern Question concerned the decline of the Ottoman Empire in eastern Europe. It was handled badly by Disraeli's government and, in 1876, Gladstone seized upon the massacre of Bulgarian citizens by Turkish troops to whip up public feelings. In the end Disraeli managed to help bring peace at the Congress of Berlin in 1878.* (3 marks)

Total for exercise: 27 marks

Exercise 9.5

1. *Victoria describes Disraeli's expression as 'disagreeable' and says that 'He has a bland manner', indicating that she was not very impressed with him.* (2 marks)

2. *Victoria realises that Disraeli's action gives Britain 'complete security for India' and describes it as 'an immense thing', clearly showing that she is impressed.* (3 marks)

3. *Source C shows Victoria giving Disraeli the title Lord Beaconsfield and therefore supports Source B, in which Victoria is also pleased with Disraeli. However, it does not agree with Source A, as A is critical of Disraeli.* **(7 marks)**

4. A good answer will look at all the sources and refer to both their content and provenance. It should cover the following points:

    ● *All of these sources are useful in understanding Disraeli's relationship with Queen Victoria.*

    ● *Sources A and B are both from Victoria's own journal; A shows their earlier relationship and B indicates that Victoria's opinion of Disraeli has improved.*

    ● *Source C is less personal, but is a contemporary source showing that many of the public saw how pleased Victoria and Disraeli were with each other.* **(8 marks)**

    Total for exercise: 20 marks

Exercise 9.6

1. Both of these essays should show a clear chronological narrative and be more than a list of events.

    (a) A good description of the life of Queen Victoria will pick out the key moments in her life, such as breaking free from her mother and her relationships with Prince Albert and men like Gladstone and Disraeli. It should cover the following points:

    ● *Victoria was born in 1819, the only living grandchild of George III.*

    ● *She became Queen on 20th June, 1837, aged 18, on the death of her uncle, William IV.*

    ● *Victoria met her Cousin, Prince Albert of Saxe-Coburg when they were both 16. In October 1939 she proposed marriage and Albert accepted.*

    ● *In 1839, Lord Melbourne lost a key vote in Parliament and resigned, leading to the Bedchamber Crisis.*

    ● *For two decades, Disraeli and Gladstone fought political battles that brought the Conservative and Liberal parties in and out of power. Victoria considered Gladstone a difficult man; Disraeli worked hard to become her favourite.*

    ● *Prince Albert died in 1861. Victoria shut herself away from the public, although she continued to go through the government papers sent to her.*

    ● *Victoria celebrated her Diamond Jubilee in 1887.*

    ● *She died in 1901.* **(20 marks)**

(b) A good description of the career of a Prime Minister (Peel, Gladstone or Disraeli) during the Victorian period should pick out key events or moments in his political career. (20 marks)

2. Both of these essays require an analytical approach and should create and explain an argument rather than simply telling the story or listing factors.

(a) The explanation of why Queen Victoria was important during her reign, and the repercussions of her reign today, could pick out the most important reason for Victoria's importance.

- *The young Victoria was lively and intelligent, and favourably impressed those around her when she became queen.*

- *Disraeli created the title 'Empress of India' for Victoria, partly to strengthen ties with India, but partly to gain favour with the queen.*

- *Following Albert's death, Victoria shut herself away from the public and saved most of the money given yearly to her, creating the wealth that the royal family enjoys to this day.* (10 marks)

(b) The assessment of the successes and failures of a Prime Minister during the Victorian period could take the form of a comparison. (10 marks)

Total for exercise: 60 marks

Chapter 10 The rise and rise of the British Empire

Exercise 10.1

As early as the **16th** century, English merchants had arrived in India, wanting to trade in goods like **spices**, **cloth**, **tea** and **silk**. The British **East India** Company was set up to organise this trade. Because the greatest power in India, the **Mughal Empire**, was in decline, the British became the dominant power, although the **French** East India Company tried to stop them. When Robert **Clive** defeated the **Nawab of Bengal** and his French allies at the Battle of **Plassey** the British began to actually rule parts of India. The problem was that the Company was created for trade and to make **money**, not to gather **taxes** and make **diplomatic** agreements. Company employees became more interested in **wealth** and returning **home** rather than in the Indian **culture** and tried to create little patches of **Britain**. This led many Indians to **distrust** the Company. Yet the British depended upon Indian soldiers, called **sepoys**, to make up most of the Company's armies. (20 marks)

Exercise 10.2

The East India Company: *The East India Company was established in 1600 to make money by trading with India. Following the British victory at the Battle of Plassey, its role developed to involve the running of Bengal, gathering taxes, administering justice and supporting its rule with military force. Over time, the Company took control of more and more of India.*
(3 marks)

Robert Clive: *The British commander Robert Clive went to India to make his fortune. In 1757 he won a great victory against the Nawab of Bengal and his French allies at the Battle of Plassey, and arranged for the East India Company to take over the running of Bengal.*
(3 marks)

Sepoys: *In order to retain control of India, the East India Company relied on local men, known as sepoys, who were recruited into the Company army to be trained and equipped in European methods of warfare. In 1857, rebellion among the sepoys led to the Indian mutiny.*
(3 marks)

The Enfield rifle and cartridges: *In 1857, the sepoys were issued with new styles of paper cartridges for their rifles. The cartridges had to be bitten to release the gunpowder inside before the rifle could be loaded. To keep the powder dry, the paper was greased with tallow,* a grease made from pork and cow fat. Since the pig is considered unclean by Muslims and the cow is sacred to Hindus, no sepoys wanted to bite the cartridges. The Company changed the type of grease used, but many sepoys believe the old type was still being supplied. (3 marks)

Mangal Pandey: Pandey was a sepoy in the 34th Native Infantry who, on 29th March 1857, stepped out of the ranks during a parade and shot at a British officer, but hit a horse instead. He was arrested and executed for mutiny and, because other sepoys in his regiment voiced their support for Pandey, the regiment was disbanded and the men lost their jobs, adding to discontent among the sepoys.   (3 marks)

The Cawnpore Massacre: Nana Sahib, an Indian prince who had lost his position because of the British East India Company, laid siege to Cawnpore with a force of mutineers and rebels. General Sir Hugh Wheeler surrendered after Nana Sahib promised safe passage by boat to a British garrison at Allahabad, but as the soldiers and civilians embarked, they were attacked. Within minutes, all 300 British soldiers and 400 civilians were dead; 200 women and children survived and were imprisoned. British troops from Allahabad then defeated Nana Sahib's force just outside Cawnpore, but when they marched into the town they found that the women and children had been killed.   (3 marks)

General Havelock: Havelock led the British column that defeated Nana Sahib's force at Cawnpore, and again at Bithur. He marched on to try to help the British at Lucknow, but was forced back to wait for reinforcements. When he finally reached the British Residency in Lucknow, he was unable to evacuate its occupants because there were too many sick and wounded, and he and his men joined the besieged. He later died from sickness.   (3 marks)

Lucknow: When news arrived of the outbreak of the rebellion, Sir Henry Lawrence gathered all the British civilians into the fortified British Residency and laid in large stocks of food. He avoided a massacre, but Lucknow was under siege for more than five months; food supplies ran low, and diseases such as smallpox and cholera broke out. When Lawrence was killed by enemy fire on 2nd July, Brigadier John Inglis took over command. On 25th September a relieving force under Havelock fought its way into Lucknow, but was unable to evacuate the many sick and wounded, and Thomas Kavanagh, dressed as a sepoy, carried a message asking for another relief force. On 17th November, Sir Colin Campbell marched into Lucknow with 4,000 men and ended the siege.   (3 marks)

Delhi: The rebellion started at Meerut, just north of Delhi, when 85 sepoys refused to use their cartridges and were put in prison, leading to riot. The sepoys then marched to Delhi, where they and three other regiments marched to the palace of the Mughal Emperor and proclaimed him their leader, before killing any British people nearby and seizing weapons and gunpowder. Delhi became the centre of the uprising. The British regained control of Delhi on 19th September, after six days of bitter fighting.   (3 marks)

Bahadur Shah II: *The 82-year-old Bahadur Shah II was the Mughal emperor when the sepoys marched into Delhi in May 1857, and was proclaimed their leader. After Delhi was retaken in September, he was caught with his family trying to flee and taken into captivity.*

(3 marks)

Total for exercise: 30 marks

Exercise 10.3

1. *The author feels revulsion and 'deep hatred' for 'the Nana', who ordered the massacre, and for the Indian people ('all his fellow race').* (2 marks)

2. *The writer was concerned that the sepoys' loyalty ('fidelty') might have been shaken by the mutineers' claim that 'the English were beaten all over India', especially since reinforcements were slow to come ('the delay in obtaining relief'). He is also aware that, had the mutineers succeeded in taking the Residency ('had the enemy carried our position'), the sepoys would have suffered badly ('the poor natives would have probably been more tortured than the Europeans').* (3 marks)

3. *The cartoon shows a tiger, representing the revolting Indians, attacking women and children, and so supports Source A in depicting the Indians as cruel and violent. However, it does not support Source B, which describes some Indian sepoys, who fought alongside the British, as loyal and brave.* (7 marks)

4. A good answer will look at all the sources, and refer to both their content and provenance. It should cover the following points:

   - *Source A, a contemporary account by a British officer who visited the site of the Cawnpore Massacre, clearly conveys the disgust felt by the British in India at the actions of the sepoy mutineers. It does not distinguish between the sepoy mutineers and those sepoys who remained loyal to the British, who played a very different role.*

   - *Source B is very useful in that it directly refers to the sepoys fighting at Lucknow and was written by an eyewitness, Captain Anderson.*

   - *Source C helps us learn something about the contemporary British response to the Mutiny and what happened at Cawnpore, but gives no information about the role of sepoys.*

   - *All three sources are written from a British point of view; there is no source from the sepoys themselves.* (8 marks)

5. A good answer will again look at all the sources and refer to both their content and provenance. It should cover the following points: (8 marks)

- *Sources A and C show that the British, both in India and at home, were outraged by the mutiny and saw the Indians as cruel and murderous.*

- *Source B tells us that some British people had a high opinion of the sepoys, who remained loyal. However, although B is an eyewitness account and therefore likely to be accurate, it would have had less effect on public opinion than propaganda such as Source C.*

- *Overall, the sources are more useful to a historian studying British opinion towards the Indian population than to someone studying the role of the sepoys.*

Total for exercise: 28 marks

Exercise 10.4

1. Both of these essays should show a strong grasp of the chronology of the events described and should evaluate the key events and/or how events are linked.

(a) A good description of the events that led to the outbreak of the Indian mutiny of 1857 should cover the following points:

- *At the beginning of the 19th century, the British in India were largely concerned with creating wealth and going home, and interest in Indian culture waned. They created little pockets of 'Britain', leading to misunderstandings with the local people.*

- *The East India Company depended on Indian soldiers, or sepoys, to help them keep control. In 1857 a new type of paper cartridge for rifles was introduced, which had to be bitten to release the gunpowder. The sepoys did not want to bite the cartridges because the paper was greased with tallow, made from pork and cow fat. The Company quickly began to use a different type of grease, but some sepoys believed the old type was still being supplied.*

- *On 29th March 1857, Mangal Pandey, a sepoy in the 34th Native Infantry, was executed and his regiment disbanded after he shot at a British officer, fuelling discontent among the sepoys.*

- *The rebellion started in earnest on 9th May, in Meerut, north of Delhi, when 85 sepoys refused to use their cartridges and were put in prison. The next day, 2,000 sepoys attacked the prison to release the prisoners. They then marched to Delhi and, with three other regiments, marched to the palace of the Mughal emperor and proclaimed him their leader.*

- *The British were taken by surprise by the outbreaks of violence. At Delhi, Lucknow and Cawnpore, large numbers of British soldiers and civilians were put under siege by the mutineers.*

(20 marks)

(b) A good description of an important event during the Indian mutiny, such as the fall of Cawnpore and the massacres, the attack on Delhi or the siege of Lucknow should identify a key moment or show some awareness of cause and effect.   (20 marks)

2. Both of these essays require an analytical approach.

(a) The explanation of the most important reason that the Indian mutiny of 1857 broke out should be more than simply a repeat of the narrative from question 1 (a) or a list of causes. A good essay will pick out one reason and then show why it is the most important, linking other factors to it. It should cover the following points:

● *The lack of interest in Indian culture among the British in India led to misunderstandings and distrust between the local people and their British overlords.*

● *Changes to the terms and pay of sepoys were unpopular.*

● *The problems over the new paper cartridges, greased with tallow, showed a lack of cultural understanding on the part of the East India Company and fuelled disquiet among the sepoys.*

● *The independent Indian rulers in the north of India became convinced that the Company wanted to seize their lands, as it had already done in some smaller states.*

● *Landowners in Bengal resented having to pay higher taxes to the British than they had done before.*

● *Many peasants feared that the British intended to force them to become Christians.*

● *The disbanding of the 34th Native Infantry, following the attempted shooting of a British officer by Mangal Pandey, put the men out of work, and other sepoys thought this very harsh.*   (10 marks)

(b) The explanation of the consequences of the Indian mutiny of 1857 should categorise the consequences as short and long-term. A good essay will also show how the consequences link to each other. It should cover the following points:

● *Following the mutiny, the British government moved quickly to strip the East India Company of its powers and wealth.*

- *The government held an inquiry into the causes of the uprising and, as a result, reformed the civil and military administrations in those areas ruled by Britain.*

- *The army was reorganised to allow locals to gain higher promotions and to ensure that British officers mixed more with their men.*

- *More British regiments were stationed in India.*

- *Civilian government was opened up to allow Indians to be promoted to higher levels.*

- *Christian missionaries were no longer encouraged, although they were still tolerated, and local temples and mosques received new recognition.*

- *The Indian rulers still independent of Britain were treated with new respect and efforts to take their lands ceased.*

- *The Mughal emperor was dethroned and sent into exile in Burma. His title was later given to Queen Victoria, who became Empress of India.* (10 marks)

Total for exercise: 60 marks

Exercise 10.5

The British Empire in 1897	covered a quarter of the world's land mass.
At Colenso	General Buller's men were stopped by the Boers under Louis Botha.
Men like Smuts and Botha	continued fighting a guerrilla war.
Alfred Milner	as High Commissioner helped push the Boer states into war.
The Boers tried to win the war quickly	by isolating and destroying the outnumbered British.
At Spion Kop	the British were forced to retreat after a vicious all-day battle.
Cecil Rhodes	dreamed of controlling as much of Africa as possible for Britain.
The Transvaal	became independent in 1881 by defeating British forces.
The railways	allowed the British to move supplies and gave the Boers an easy target to attack.

The British began to win	when Lord Roberts took command.
At Magersfontein	the British fell into a trap and were defeated.
The Great Trek	was an attempt by the Boers to escape British control.
The Boers accepted the annexation of Transvaal in 1877	because they felt threatened by the Zulus.
The fall of Pretoria	seemed to mean the end of the war.
Lord Kitchner's ruthless campaign	finally wore down the Boers in 1901.

(15 marks)

Exercise 10.6

Afrikaners: *The Dutch settlers in South Africa were known as Boers or Afrikaners. When South Africa was seized by the British during the Napoleonic Wars, many Afrikaners travelled northwards, where they came into conflict with both the local people and the Zulus.*

(3 marks)

Cecil Rhodes: *Rhodes controlled the large diamond mining company de Beers and made his fortune in diamonds in South Africa. He was committed to British Imperialism and, after becoming Governor of Cape Colony, annexed two areas north of the Boers, which were named Northern and Southern Rhodesia in his honour (now Zambia and Zimbabwe). In 1896, he tried to stir up a rebellion among the Uitlanders, but the raid failed and he had to give up the governorship of Cape Colony.*

(3 marks)

President Paul Kruger: *Kruger was president of the Transvaal. He resisted the right to vote being granted to Uitlanders, which played straight into the hands of those British who wished to annexe the Transvaal; he then clashed with Alfred Milner, the High Commissioner for South Africa. Believing that the British were not well led and were easy to defeat in battle, in 1899 he sent an ultimatum demanding that the British troops on their way to South Africa never land and all British troops on the borders with the Transvaal be removed; this allowed Britain to declare war, telling the British public that the Boers were the aggressors.*

(3 marks)

The Jameson raid: *When gold was discovered in the southern Transvaal, the town of Johannesburg sprang up and was populated by thousands of outsiders, or Uitlanders. The Boers welcomed the money produced, but kept political control in their own hands. In 1896 Cecil Rhodes sent 500 men, under his friend Dr. Leander Jameson, to try to stir up a rebellion among the Uitlanders, but the raid failed.*

(3 marks)

Boer commandos: *The Boers found in commandos, groups of mounted soldiers who moved swiftly over the veld grasslands of South Africa. Their knowledge of the land and intense desire to defend their homeland made them formidable opponents for the British.* (3 marks)

Mafeking: *In 1899, the Boer's swift offensive caught the British forces off guard, and the British force at Mafeking found itself under siege. The siege became a symbol of British resolve: its commander, Colonel Robert Baden-Powell held out with a force of only 1,000 men, many of them volunteers, until he was relieved on 17th May, after 217 days.* (3 marks)

General Buller: *British General Sir Redvers Buller arrived in South Africa at the end of October, 1899. He sent part of his army to Kimberley and Mafeking, and planned to use the rest to save Ladysmith, before marching into the Transvaal and the Orange Free State. However, on his way to Ladysmith, he was bloodily repulsed by the Boers at Colenso. This and other British defeats during 'Black Week' led to his removal from overall command in South Africa.* (3 marks)

Magersfontein: *The Boers defeated the British at Magersfontein by laying a trap. Lord Methuen believed that the Boers would defend a line of small hills, and concentrated his artillery fire on them before the British infantry attacked; in fact, the Boer General Koos De la Ray had hidden his 8,000 men in concealed trenches in front of the hills. When the advancing British infantry were just 265m from the trenches, the Boers unleashed a great sheet of rifle fire. The British dived for cover and stayed pinned down for nine hours, before breaking and running.* (3 marks)

Colenso: *General Buller and the British were defeated at Colenso by the best Afrikaner general of the war, Louis Botha. He had turned the Tugela River, 16km south of Ladysmith, into a giant moat, with defensive trenches on the northern bank. Buller attacked but was bloodily repulsed.* (3 marks)

Spion Kop: *After the British defeat at Colenso, Buller and the newly arrived General Warren decided to try to break through to Ladysmith by taking Spion Kop, a 400m hill. On the night of 23rd January 1900, nearly 2,000 British troops climbed the hill and drove off the few Boer defenders. However, at dawn they found themselves surrounded by Boers on the neighbouring, higher hills. After a vicious all-day battle, the British retreated, although the Boers were also close to breaking point.* (3 marks)

Sir Frederick Sleigh (Lord Roberts): *Lord Roberts arrived in South Africa in early January 1900, to replace General Buller. He came to South Africa with a larger and better-equipped army and soon showed that he had learned different ideas on fighting from his campaigns in Afghanistan and Abyssinia. Rather than attacking the Boers head on, he used his mounted forces to encircle and trap them. On 15th February he reached Kimberly, ending the 124-day siege, and on 27th February he forced Cronje to surrender. The Orange Free State's capital of Bloemfontein fell to his forces, and on 5th June he entered the Transvaal capital of Pretoria.*

(3 marks)

Paardeberg: Lord Roberts' tactics forced Cronje and his men to abandon their lines at Magersfontein and attempt to escape towards Bloemfontein, but the British cavalry caught up with them and trapped them at Paardeberg. The Boers entrenched a hill and fought off British attacks, but Boer General De la Rey was unable to break through to help Conje, and Conje surrendered on 27th February 1900.

(3 marks)

Guerrilla warfare: After the fall of Pretoria, about 25,000 Boers still bore arms. Led by young, determined commanders, such as Jan Smuts and Louis Botha, they engaged in guerrilla warfare, launching attacks, then vanishing into the vast landscape to reform and attack again. They continually attacked the railway lines, which the British needed to move troops and supplies around the country. They even managed to raid Cape Colony. However, the British destroyed Boer farms, livestock and crops, and by 1901 the remaining commandos were out of supplies.

(3 marks)

Concentration camps: The concentration camps were established by the British as part of their attempt to stop the guerrilla war. Women and children were crammed into tents with little clothing, food or provision for hygiene or sanitation. The conditions were totally inadequate for the number of people brought to the camps and the death rate was high, particularly among children.

(3 marks)

Lord Kitchener: Kitchener took charge of the British troops in South Africa when Lord Roberts left in December 1900 to become Commander-in-Chief of the British Army. He carried on Roberts' policies, but with greater ruthlessness, giving the order to starve out the Boer guerrillas by destroying Boer farms and forcing the women and children into concentration camps.

(3 marks)

Total for exercise: 45 marks

Exercise 10.7

1. The writer is worried about the 'frightening mortality' in the concentration camps. He says that while there may be 'a hundred explanations' and 'a hundred excuses', the deaths in the camps are indefensible for the British government. (2 marks)

2. The Boer women are worried about illness among the children in the camps. The source speaks of the 'sufferings of their undernourished children' and notes that, among the sick, 'a disproportionate number … were children'. (3 marks)

3. Source C agrees with Source B in that both emphasise the number of women and children in the camps, but gives a good impression of conditions within the camps, whereas Sources A and B both claim that conditions were extremely poor.　(7 marks)

4. A good answer will look at all the sources and refer to both their content and provenance. It should cover the following points:

    - Source A is the only contemporary source that admits there is a problem in the camps. Written by a British eyewitness, the High Commissioner Alfred Milner, it is likely to be accurate.

    - Source B is a later source, but reflects the judgement of a modern historian who has examined the contemporary evidence and is therefore likely to be accurate.

    - Source C is a contemporary source, but was taken to reassure the husbands and fathers of the women and children in the Bethulie Concentration Camp of their proper care by British authorities. It is therefore propaganda and reflects the message the British authorities wanted to send rather than the truth of the situation.
    　(8 marks)

5. A good answer will again look at all the sources and refer to both their content and provenance. It should cover the following points:

    - Source A is a contemporary response to the camps and shows what some within the government fear might be the public reaction, but does not tell us anything about actual public opinion at the time.

    - Source B, being a later source, tells us only the views of the Boer women and does not tell us about the contemporary British reaction.

    - Source C is contemporary propaganda and could be seen as an attempt to cover over any real problems.
    　(8 marks)

    Total for exercise: 28 marks

Exercise 10.8

1. Both of these essays should show a strong grasp of the chronology of the events described.

    (a) A good description of a British defeat during the Boer War will show how factors/events are linked; for example, British underestimation of the Boers, poor planning and lack of knowledge of the terrain played significant roles in the defeats.
    　(20 marks)

(b) A good description of the role of one commander during the Boer War could either assess the chosen general's overall success or failure or identify the key decisions or events in his Boer War career. (20 marks)

2. Both of these essays require an analytical approach.

(a) The explanation of the most important reason for the outbreak of the Boer War should include a reasoned argument as to why the chosen reason was the most important; the more this can be tied in to other reasons, the more effective the argument becomes. (10 marks)

(b) The explanation of who won the Boer War and why could contrast two points of view: one that the British were the clear winners and the other that in the long run the Boers were the more successful. Alternatively, the consequences of the war could be examined and categorised as short or long-term. (10 marks)

Total for exercise: 60 marks

Appendix

Essay questions: generic mark scheme

Selective description

e.g. Describe the key features of … etc.

Mark	Target	Causation/recall of knowledge
1–8	Level 1	Simple statements offering some features/ideas supported by some knowledge; embryonic, inaccurate or irrelevant knowledge; lacking real coherence and structure.
9–15	Level 2	More developed statements giving features supported by more relevant knowledge; thinly substantiated passages; uncertain overall structure.
16–20	Level 3	Developed selection of features with sound substantiation and structure; good range of features; for top of level, answer will show clear linkage and relevant importance of features.

Evaluation / Analysis

e.g. Explain why …

Mark	Target	Evaluation of factors against one another/definitions of success and failure/contextual assessment
1–4	Level 1	Simple statement offering basic and largely unfocused opinion.
5–8	Level 2	More developed analysis with some coherent judgement; some substantiation of assertions.
9–10	Level 3	Precisely selected knowledge in a clear framework of argument; strong and developed analysis/assessment with cogent judgements; strong substantiation of assertions.

Evidence questions: mark scheme (total: 25 marks)

Mark	Target	Comprehension of source
1	Level 1	Incomplete or imprecise answer.
2	Level 2	Answer which more clearly substantiates from the source.

Mark	Target	Comprehension of source
1	Level 1	Incomplete or imprecise answer.
2–3	Level 2	More developed understanding.

Mark	Target	Corroboration by cross-referencing sources
1	Level 1	Simple statement which makes a basic comment on a source.
2–4	Level 2	Answer which is more developed, connecting Source C to another source with a substantiated argument.
5–6	Level 3	Fully developed answer which examines all three sources using a substantiated argument.

Mark	Target	Evaluation of sources for utility/consideration of provenance
1–2	Level 1	Simple statement which makes a basic comment on a source, looking only at the content.
3–5	Level 2	Answer which recognises that different sources can be useful for different purposes. For lower reaches of this band, relies on generalised comments, such as 'it depends on what you want to know' or 'all sources are useful in one way or another'.
6	Level 3	Developed and substantiated analysis of all three sources, looking at both content and provenance, and contextual appreciation that they all, in their own way, help our understanding of the argument.

Mark	Target	Making a judgement about an interpretation, relating analysis of sources to contextual knowledge
1–3	**Level 1**	Answer which makes little or no use of sources or makes little or no use of own knowledge. There is poor argument, little or no substantiation and only vague/embryonic statement of agreement/disagreement.
4–6	**Level 2**	More developed answer, making better use of sources in terms of content and with some own knowledge. *Or* good use of own knowledge but weaker use of sources.
7–8	**Level 3**	Answer which makes full and intelligent use of all three sources, examining content and interleaving answer with accurate and pertinent own knowledge. For top of this level, the candidate will have written a very cogent and well-structured answer, with judicious appreciation of the sources and own knowledge in equal measure.